# Basic Japanese Grammar

Everett F. Bleiler

**TUTTLE** Publishing

Tokyo | Rutland, Vermont | Singapore

## "Books to Span the East and West"

**Tuttle Publishing** was founded in 1832 in the small New England town of Rutland, Vermont [USA]. Our core values remain as strong today as they were then—to publish best-in-class books which bring people together one page at a time. In 1948, we established a publishing office in Japan—and Tuttle is now a leader in publishing English-language books about the arts, languages and cultures of Asia. The world has become a much smaller place today and Asia's economic and cultural influence has grown. Yet the need for meaningful dialogue and information about this diverse region has never been greater. Over the past seven decades, Tuttle has published thousands of books on subjects ranging from martial arts and paper crafts to language learning and literature—and our talented authors, illustrators, designers and photographers have won many prestigious awards. We welcome you to explore the wealth of information available on Asia at **www.tuttlepublishing.com**.

Published by Tuttle Publishing, an imprint of Periplus Editions (HK) Ltd.

**www.tuttlepublishing.com**

Copyright © 1963 by Charles E. Tuttle Publishing Company, Inc.
This revised edition © 2011 by Periplus Editions (HK) Ltd.

This work was originally published in the United States under the title *Essential Japanese Grammar* by Dover Publications, Inc.

LCC Card Number: 2010033404
ISBN 978-4-8053-1143-1

23 22 21    11 10 9    2111VP
Printed in Malaysia

TUTTLE PUBLISHING® is a registered trademark of Tuttle Publishing, a division of Periplus Editions (HK) Ltd.

**Distributed by:**

**North America, Latin America & Europe**
Tuttle Publishing
364 Innovation Drive, North Clarendon,
VT 05759-9436 U.S.A
Tel: 1 (802) 773 8930
Fax: 1 (802) 773 6993
info@tuttlepublishing.com
www.tuttlepublishing.com

**Japan**
Tuttle Publishing
Yaekari Bldg., 3rd Floor
5-4-12 Osaki, Shinagawa-ku
Tokyo 141 0032
Tel: (81) 3 5437 0171
Fax: (81) 3 5437 0755
sales@tuttle.co.jp
www.tuttle.co.jp

**Asia Pacific**
Berkeley Books Pte. Ltd.
3 Kallang Sector
#04-01, Singapore 349278
Tel: (65) 6741 2178
Fax: (65) 6741 2179
inquiries@periplus.com.sg
www.tuttlepublishing.com

# Contents

# How To Use This Book

*Basic Japanese Grammar* assumes that you will be spending a limited number of hours studying Japanese grammar and that your objective is simple everyday communication. It is offered not as a condensed outline of all aspects of Japanese grammar, but as a series of aids that will enable you to use more effectively and with greater versatility phrases and vocabulary that you have previously learned. It will familiarize you with the more common structure and patterns of the language.

If this is your first introduction to Japanese grammar, the following suggestions may be helpful.

1. Don't approach *Basic Japanese Grammar* until you have mastered many useful phrases and expressions such as you will find in any good phrase book or audio course.

2. Start at the beginning of this book and read through it. Look up unfamiliar or confusing grammatical terms in the short glossary in the rear. Don't be concerned if sections are not immediately clear to you. On second or third reading they will make better sense. What may appear discouragingly difficult at first will become understandable as your studies progress. As you use the language and hear it spoken, many aspects of Japanese grammar will begin to form recognizable patterns.

3. Go back to *Basic Japanese Grammar* periodically. Sections that seem difficult or of doubtful benefit to you now may prove extremely helpful later.

4. For the most part, *Basic Japanese Grammar* is presented in a logical order, especially for the major divisions of grammar,

and you will do best if you follow its sequence in your studies. However, the author is aware that some students learn best when they study to answer their immediate questions and needs (e.g. how to form the comparative; the conjugation of the verb *to be*, etc.). If you prefer to work in this manner, study entire sections rather than isolated parts.

# Introductory Material

## Introduction to the Japanese Language

Japanese, unlike the other foreign languages that you are likely to have studied, is not a member of the Indo-European family, and is not related to English. Nor is it related to Chinese, even though it has borrowed a large vocabulary from Chinese. It is pretty much a language by itself, although it may be related to Korean, and some philologists believe that in the far distant past it had a common ancestor with certain Central Asiatic languages that are called Altaic. But these possible relationships are remote, and can be appreciated only by comparative philologists.

As a result of this linguistic distance from English, Japanese grammar is very different from English grammar. This difference is not just a question of different forms and endings, as is often the case between English and German or French or Spanish or Russian; it is frequently a question of a different classification of human experience. You must be prepared when you study Japanese grammar to suspend your ideas of what the parts of speech are and how they are used, what a sentence is and how it is constructed, how ideas are expressed and how variations on these ideas are indicated. As you read through this manual, do not limit yourself to memorizing the construction of forms and idea-equations between English and Japanese. Try also to understand the psychology of language that lies behind this often very different way of talking about experience. You will find this very broadening, for you soon learn that many of the standards that you hold (consciously or unconsciously) about language are not necessary. You will be surprised to discover that many of the concepts that we consider indispensable to "sense" can be stripped away and discarded, with no real loss to meaning.

In some ways Japanese is simpler than English, and in other ways it is more complex. It can be extremely simple in its expression of basic ideas, yet very elaborate in expressing the speaker's feeling about the ideas. The conversational situation affects expression more than it does in English, and forms of courtesy enter much more than they do in European languages. Japanese is extremely regular in its grammatical forms; the exceptions to the grammatical rules of formation can be counted on your fingers. On the other hand, syntax and sentence structure can become very complex, and idioms are numerous.

This manual does not provide a complete coverage of Japanese grammar, but has been limited to constructions that are indispensable to either comprehension or ordinary simple speech. We have omitted many verb forms that you probably would not hear very often, and we have presented a very small number of special constructions and idioms. Where there is a choice among several ways of expressing an idea—which is often the case in Japanese—we have tried to create a balance between the most commonly used Japanese forms and the forms that are easiest for an American to master. This is not baby Japanese, however, or kitchen Japanese, or any other pidgin language that has grown up among foreigners who do not care to learn correct Japanese. It is just the simpler, basic aspect of modern colloquial Japanese. While you may find a more complex Japanese (with, at times, different forms and constructions than we give) in books, periodicals, and newspapers, this book teaches the standard colloquial Japanese that is understood anywhere in Japan.

As we have already said, Japanese grammar does not always parallel English grammar, and it would be a distortion to present Japanese in terms of English forms or ideas. It would be equally inadvisable to present it in the system that native Japanese grammarians follow, or in the technical analysis of a comparative philologist. Instead, we have tried to present a descriptive grammar that can be easily followed by an English speaker, yet does not depart from the spirit of the language. The English terminology for Japanese grammar, unfortunately, has not yet been standardized, so that constructions may be called by many different names according to the grammar book that one uses. Our approach to this problem has been eclectic: we have selected the term that seems to fit the situation best and seems to be the most meaningful to an English speaker. We have often mentioned other terminologies, however, so that you will not be at a loss if you continue on to more advanced grammars.

## Notation

Beneath each Japanese sentence we have supplied a literal word-for-word translation of the sentence. In some cases this can be only approximate, since there is no real word-for-word correspondence between the two languages, but it will still indicate to you the grammatical processes involved and the psychology of language behind the grammar and syntax.

To keep the parallelism exact, we have often hyphenated the English literal translation, so that you can identify correspondences. The Japanese word **wa**, for example, we have translated literally as "as-for," so that by the English you can understand that a single word is involved in Japanese. In most cases English is more verbose than Japanese, and it is only rarely that two Japanese words must be translated by a single English word. Such a case is the Japanese sequence **no de**, which we translate as "since" or "because." To retain the word-for-word parallelism, we have inserted a long dash in the English. You need not worry about this, since it occurs in only two or three places.

Grammatical processes occur in Japanese for which there are no English translations. In such cases we have made use of the following arbitrary English abbreviations to indicate the Japanese meaning:

*subj* (which is normally placed under the Japanese word **ga** in our literal translation) indicates that the preceding word is the subject of the clause or sentence.

*obj* (which is normally placed under the Japanese word **o** in our literal translation) indicates the preceding word is the direct object of the verb.

*ques* (which is normally placed under the Japanese word **ka** in our literal translation) is equivalent to a question mark. It indicates that the sentence is a question.

*hon* indicates that something has been inserted into a sentence or has been added to a word to express respect. It has no literal lexical meaning, but is part of the linguistic etiquette of the language. For example, the word **tegami** would normally be translated as "letter"; the word **otegami**, however, also means "letter," but the prefix **o-** indicates a certain feeling of courtesy or respect that we cannot translate into English (though in cartoon-strip Japanese-English this would be translated as "your honorable letter"). To indicate the presence of this honorific (for a full discussion see page 113), we translate **otegami** literally as "*hon-*letter," and in the colloquial English translation as simply "letter."

The colloquial English translation that appears below the literal translation is somewhat arbitrary in many cases, since it reflects what might be expected in a normal conversational situation. In most cases other translations could be equally valid. You will appreciate this point after you have worked through this grammar.

## Basic Japanese

You may not have the time to work through this series of grammatical aids. For an acquaintance with the absolute minimum of Japanese grammar, we suggest that you read the following sections:

With a command of this material you should be able to express most simple statements, even though you will not be able to express any complexity of thought. You should also be able to understand the grammatical situations in most simple statements that may be made to you. We advise you, however, to advance beyond these sections, if possible. Japanese grammar, though different from your past experience, is not really difficult, and a knowledge of basic forms and concepts will greatly enlarge your ability to understand and to express yourself, and will make your travel more pleasant.

## General Information
In this section we shall anticipate the more detailed explanations that follow in the remainder of this book, and shall give you a brief summary of important points of Japanese grammar that are likely to be strange to you. Bear these points in mind as you work through the rest of these hints, and you will probably be able to understand the general structure of Japanese better and to follow the speech patterns in the sentences and phrases that we give as examples.

1. There are no words corresponding to the English words *a*, *an*, or *the*.
2. Nouns do not have special plural forms; they remain the same whether they indicate one object or many. The Japanese word **to**, for example, can mean "a door," "the door," "doors," or "the doors."
3. Pronouns are usually omitted if they can be understood from the context. But they can be used for emphasis, or when they are needed to make the meaning clear.

Ex.　**Ikaga desu ka?**　　　　**Genki desu.**
　　いくらですか。　　　　元気です。
　　[how is *ques*]　　　　　[good-health is]
　　How are you?　　　　　I am fine, thank you.

　　**Kare wa, hon ga kaitai?**
　　彼は、本が買いたい？
　　[he as-for book *subj* buying-wishing *ques*]
　　Does he want to buy a book?

4. Verbs do not have special forms to indicate person or number. Each tense has only one form, which is used no matter what the subject is. **Yomu** (to read), for example, could be the form used to translate the word *read* in any of these situations: I read, you read, he reads, we read, they read, the man reads, and so on.

5. True Japanese adjectives are closely related to verbs, and take endings according to their tense and mood. You use the dictionary form when an adjective modifies a noun.

6. There are no cases for nouns or pronouns. Relationships between the words of a sentence are indicated by little words called particles or postpositions, which are placed after the word they control. The most common are: **ga**, which usually indicates the subject of a clause; **wa**, which can be translated as "as-for" and often indicates the subject of a clause; **o**, which follows the direct object; **no**, which means "of" in most of the English senses of the word, and indicates possession; and **ka**, which indicates a question.

Ex. **Kisha ga kimasu.**　　**Kyō wa ii tenki desu.**
汽車が来ます。　　　今日はいい天気です。
[train *subj* comes]　　[today as-for good weather is]
The train comes.　　　The weather is fine today.

**Watashi wa sore o mimasu.**
私はそれを見ます。
[I as-for that *obj* see]
I see it.

**Anata wa gakusei desu ka?**
あなたは学生ですか。
[you as-for student is *ques*]
Are you a student?

7. The frequent endings -**masu**, -**mashita**, and -**mashō** are verb endings. They indicate, respectively, the present tense, the past tense, and a peculiarly Japanese mode which is usually translated by using the word *probably* in the sentence. The

ending -**masen** indicates a present negative verb; -**masen deshita** a past tense negative; and -**masen deshō** indicates a negative tense involving probability—"probably does not," etc. All of these are polite forms and are the forms that you are most likely to meet in ordinary conversation.

8. The common ending -**te** usually indicates a verb participle, which can be translated into English in most cases by a present participle ("-ing"): **kite**, "coming"; **aruite**, "walking"; **shite**, "doing."

9. Basic word order is subject—object—verb. Japanese is somewhat rigid with respect to word order, and verbs must come last.

   Ex.   **Watashi wa shinbun o yonde imasu.**
         私は新聞を読んでいます。
         [I as-for newspaper *obj* reading am]
         As for me, I'm reading a newspaper.

10. Conjunctions come at the end of the clause they govern.

11. Subordinate clauses must come first in the sentence. You must say: If I see him, I will pay him. You cannot say: I will pay him if I see him.

Do not be disturbed or discouraged if you do not understand these situations completely or if you do not understand why certain forms have been made or used. Simply accept them for what they are. We have provided this forewarning to Japanese grammar only to give you orientation before you consider reasons and details later. Language study is all too often a spiderweb of interrelated problems, in which it is not always possible to follow one strand without disturbing other strands and invoking other equally complex situations. A fragment of background knowledge can often make your learning task much easier.

### The Language of Courtesy (Introductory)

Japanese is very rich in special forms that indicate shades of courtesy, respect, and formality that often are impossible to express in English. These forms originally demonstrated the amount of social respect or awe that the speaker felt toward the person he was addressing or toward a third party. This concept of a language of respect (which has certainly had less complex parallels in the Western world) originally arose in the highly stratified society of Imperial China, where language was often a means of retaining or enhancing one's own position by insulting inferiors and fawning upon superiors. These concepts then moved to Japan. Even today, although the social stratification that gave birth to them has been broken, these archaic forms have been frozen in place and are still customarily used, though at times to a lesser degree.

For the purpose of this brief outline of grammar we may say that there are four levels of language etiquette—although the actual number might be argued. These are (1) rude, which you might use toward inferiors or as an insult; (2) abrupt-neutral, which in some constructions is neutral in tone, and in other situations is somewhat abrupt to use toward an equal; (3) normal-polite, which you would use to your equals and perhaps your superiors; (4) very polite, which you would use to superiors. In this grammar we have restricted ourselves to abrupt-neutral (2) and normal-polite (3), which are the forms you will hear in everyday life. We have also included a few very polite forms that seem to be moving down toward normal-polite acceptance.

Since it is better if you err on the side of politeness rather than of rudeness, you will probably be safest if you use the polite forms that we stress in this series of grammatical aids. You should also use the abrupt-neutral forms in the special grammatical situations that we shall indicate. After you have spent some time in Japan and have learned the proper social situations, you can enlarge your speech level with more safety.

# Nouns

Japanese nouns have only one form, which is not changed to indicate number, gender, or the role that the noun plays within the sentence. The same form is used under all circumstances. This form also includes within itself the ideas of the English "the" and "a" (or "an"), which do not exist separately in Japanese.

猫　**neko**　a cat, the cat, the cats, cats
電車 **densha** a train, the train, the trains, trains
傘　 **kasa**　an umbrella, the umbrella, the umbrellas, umbrellas

This will probably seem very imprecise to you, and you may wonder how you are going to express your thoughts. You will soon discover that you can get along perfectly well without special plural forms, just as you do with such English words as *sheep, fish, quail,* or *deer.*

In most cases, the number of things that you are talking about will be clear from context. Where it is necessary to be specific, you can always use numbers or words indicating quantity, just as we do with the English nouns that have no separate plural form. (For the way that you use numbers with nouns, which is quite different from English, see page 125.)

**takusan no jidōsha**
たくさんの自動車
[quantity of auto]
many automobiles

# Personal Pronouns

In modern colloquial Japanese the personal pronouns are usually omitted if the meaning of the sentence is clear without them, just as is the case in Spanish or Italian.

**Ikaga desu ka?**
いかがですか。
[how are *ques*]
How are you?

**Genki desu.**
元気です。
[fine-health is]
I am fine.

When it is necessary to express a pronoun, either for emphasis or for clearness, use the words in this table:

**watashi**
私
I, me

**watashitachi**\*
私たち
we, us

**anata**
あなた
you (SING.)

**anatatachi**\*
あなたたち
you (PL.)

**kare**
彼
he, him

**karera**
彼ら
they, them (MASC.)

**kanojo**
彼女
she, her

**kanojotachi**
彼女たち
they, them (FEM.)

In addition to these normal-polite forms, Japanese is very rich in other words that convey a great variety of shades of familiarity, politeness, and formality. Most of these forms are beyond the scope of

---

\* You will also hear the forms **watashidomo** 私ども for we and **anatagata** あんたがた for you (PL.).

this manual, but you should be aware of two other personal pronouns that are very commonly used:

**boku** 僕　I, me
**kimi** 君　you

These words are less courteous and less formal than **watashi** and **anata**, and they are used in conversation between intimates and members of some social groups, such as students.

Like nouns, pronouns do not change their forms according to their use within a sentence. Thus, as the tables show, **watashi** can mean "I" or "me"; **boku** can mean "I" or "me," and so on.

We can anticipate the discussion of possessives (see page 24) to say that the pronominal adjectives are formed entirely regularly and simply by placing the word **no** after the pronoun in question.

| | | | | | |
|---|---|---|---|---|---|
| **watashi no** | 私の | my | **watashitachi no** | 私たちの | our |
| **anata no** | あなたの | your | **anatatachi no** | あなたたちの | your (PL.) |
| **kare no** | 彼の | his | **karera no** | 彼らの | their (MASC.) |
| **kanojo no** | 彼女の | her | **kanojotachi no** | 彼女たちの | their (FEM.) |
| **boku no** | 僕の | my | **kimi no** | 君の | your |

Sentences:

**Watashi no namae wa Kido desu.**
私の名前は木戸です。
[I of name as-for Kido is]
My name is Kido.

**Sore ga watakushi no desu.**
それが私のです。
[that *subj* I of is]
That is mine.

**Anata wa sensei desu ka?**
あなたは先生ですか。
[you as-for teacher are *ques*]
Are you a teacher?

**Iie. Watashi wa gakusei desu.**
いいえ、私は学生です。
[no. I as-for student am]
No, I am a student.

**Kimi to boku wa dōkyūsei desu.**
君と僕は同級生です。
[you and I as-for classmates are]
You and I are classmates.

**Karera wa watashitachi o matte imasu.**
彼らは私達を待っています。
[they as-for we *obj* waiting are]
They are waiting for us.

The impersonal pronoun *it*, in such expressions as, "It is raining," "It is Sunday," is not translated into Japanese.

**Ame ga futte imasu.**
雨が降っています。
[rain *subj* falling is]
It is raining.

**Nichiyō desu.**
日曜です。
[Sunday is]
It is Sunday.

# Using Nouns and Pronouns in Sentences

Japanese, like English, has the concepts of subject, of sentences, direct objects, and indirect objects, but it expresses these concepts in a different manner.

In English we show the relationships between the words of a sentence mostly by word order: "The policeman chased the burglar" is obviously quite different in meaning from "The burglar chased the policeman." Only in the pronouns, in English, do we have different forms or endings to show the function of a word in a sentence: *I*, *me*, *my*, *he*, *him*, *his*, *we*, *our*, and so on.

In Japanese, however, the sentence function of nouns and pronouns is shown by additional words that are placed immediately after the noun or pronoun. (Word order, which is also extremely important, will be considered later: page 121.) These words, which are called particles or postpositions, might by a stretch of the imagination be considered as acting in the same way as the case endings that you learned if you studied German or Latin, although in Japanese these particles never vary, but always remain the same.

The three most important of these signposts within a sentence are **ga**, **wa**, and **o**.

**ga** usually indicates the grammatical subject of the sentence or clause in which it appears. We specify grammatical subject because the Japanese grammatical subject is very often not the logical subject in the English translation. **ga** indicates that the immediately preceding noun or pronoun is the subject, and we indicate it in our literal translation by the symbol *subj*. Sentences:

**Ame ga harete, hi ga tette imasu.**
雨が晴れて、日が照っています。
[rain *subj* ceasing, sun *subj* shining is]
It has stopped raining, and the sun is shining.

**Atama ga itamimasu.**
頭が痛みます。
[head *subj* pains]
I have a headache.

**Yamazaki san ga kuru.**
山崎さんが来る。
[Yamazaki Mr. *subj* comes]
Mr. Yamazaki comes.

**wa** (spelled **ha** in the Japanese syllabary) indicates that the material that it immediately follows is to be set apart from the grammatical basis of the Japanese sentence. A rough English translation that will fit it in most situations is "as-for."

**Kyō wa umi ga taihen kirei desu.**
今日は海が大変きれいです。
[today as-for sea *subj* very beautiful is]
Today the sea is very beautiful.

**Boku wa ashita ongakkai ni ikimasu.**
僕はあした音楽会に行きます。
[I as-for tomorrow concert to go]
As for me, tomorrow I shall go to the concert. I shall go to the concert tomorrow.

As you may have observed in the sentences above, **wa** often indicates material that is the subject of the English translation.

**Anata wa eigo ga dekimasu ka?**
あなたは英語ができますか。
[you as-for English-language *subj* able *ques*]
Do you speak English?

You may be puzzled about when you should use **ga** to indicate the subject, and when you should use **wa**. Actually, this involves a very subtle distinction in Japanese thought, and is very difficult for a foreigner to master. This point is beyond the scope of these grammatical aids. We can say, however, that **wa** on the whole is best translated by placing emphasis on the predicate of the sentence, and **ga** by placing emphasis on the subject.

**Kare wa hikōki de kimasu.**
彼は飛行機で来ます。
[he as-for airplane by comes]
He is coming by airplane. (Emphasis on "coming by airplane")

**Kare ga hikōki de kimasu.**
彼が飛行機で来ます。
[he *subj* airplane by comes]
He is coming by airplane. (Emphasis upon "he")

It is possible for us to make these distinctions in English, but we are much less concerned with them than is Japanese.

**o** (sometimes transliterated **wo**, and spelled **wo** in the Japanese kana writing) indicates that the preceding word is the direct object of the verb. It is often used with verbs of motion that English would consider incapable of taking a direct object:

**Omiyage o kaimashita.**
お土産を買いました。
[souvenirs *obj* bought]
I (or you, or he, etc.) bought some souvenirs.

**Kōbe o tachimashita.**
神戸を発ちました。
[Kōbe *obj* left]
We (or I, or you, or he, etc.) left Kōbe.

It is very important that you understand how these postpositions are used, since they are the cement that bonds together the parts of a Japanese sentence. They cannot be omitted in a grammatically correct sentence, if nouns or pronouns are present.* You must indicate the subject of a clause by either **ga** or **wa**, and you must indicate the direct object, if there is one, by **o**.

The two common particles that are used to form questions may also be mentioned here. These are **ka** and **ne**.

**ka** is normally placed at the end of a question, and is equivalent to an English question mark. **ne**, which is also placed at the end of the sentence, is equivalent to the French *n'est-ce pas* or German *nicht wahr* or English *isn't it?* **ne** often has the feeling of an exclamation.

---

* In very colloquial speech, **wa** (and the other postpositions to a lesser extent) are occasionally omitted. But it is better if you avoid this, and use postpositions wherever they are called for.

**Kore wa nan desu ka?**

これは何ですか。

[this as-for what is *ques*]

As for this, what is it? What is this?

**Rikōna kodomo desu ne?**

りこうな子供ですね。

[intelligent child is isn't-it]

It's an intelligent child, isn't it? What an intelligent child!

**Kare wa amerika-jin desu ne?**

彼はアメリカ人ですね。

[he as-for America-man is isn't-he]

He is an American, isn't he?

# Particles Equivalent to Prepositions, Adverbs, Conjunctions

Besides the three basic particles of sentence structure (**ga**, **wa**, and **o**) and the two particles that indicate questions (**ka** and **ne**), Japanese has a very wide range of words that are equivalent in function to the English prepositions, adverbs, and conjunctions. All of these particles are placed after the word they modify, and for this reason are called *post*positions, instead of *pre*positions. We shall discuss only the most important of these secondary particles here: **no**, **to**, **ya**, **kara**, **made**, **ni**, **e**, **de**, and **mo**.

   **no** corresponds in many ways to the English preposition *of*. It can indicate:*

(1) possession, ownership, attribution.

> **Kore ga boku no kamera desu.**
> これが僕のカメラです。
> [this *subj* I of camera is]
> This is my camera.

(2) material.

> **Ki no isu desu.**
> 木の椅子です。
> [Wood of chair is]
> The chair is of wood. It is a wooden chair.

---

\* In dependent clauses, **no** is often used to indicate the subject of the clause:
   **Kore ga kare no tateta tera desu.**
   これが彼の建てた寺です。
   [this *subj* he *subj* built temple is]
   This is the temple that he built.
The Japanese dependent clause is difficult for an English speaker, and it is discussed in more detail on page 84. We mention it here only so that you will not be bewildered by this use of **no** if you come upon it.

(3) origin, time, place, apposition.

### Koko no wa mina firumu de gozaimasu.

ここのはみなフィルムでございます。

[here of as-for all film being is]

As for what's here, they are all films. There is nothing here but
film.

**to** can sometimes be translated as "with" (meaning accompaniment) and sometimes "and."

### Kondōsan to Chūshingura o mi ni ikimashita.

近藤さんと忠臣蔵を見に行きました。

[Kondō-Mr. with Chūshingura *obj* see to went]

I went with Mr. Kondō to see the Chūshingura play. Mr. Kondō and I
went to see the Chūshingura.

### Satō to shio to kome o katta.

砂糖と塩と米を買った。

[sugar and salt and rice *obj* bought]

I bought sugar and salt and rice.

**to** is not always equivalent to the English word *and*, however. **to** is
used only to link series of nouns or pronouns, and cannot be used to
link verbs or clauses.

**to** does not mean "with" in the sense of "using," or "by means of";
for this concept, another postposition, usually **de** or **ni**, is used.

**ya** is usually equivalent to the English *and*. Like **to**, however, it can
link only series of nouns or pronouns.

### Tadao ya Kiyoshi ya Shigeru ga Kōbe e ikimashita.

タダオやキヨシやシゲルが神戸へ行きました。

[Tadao and Kiyoshi and Shigeru *subj* Kōbe to went]

Tadao and Kiyoshi and Shigeru all went to Kōbe.

There is a subtle difference between **ya** and **to** in such sentences. **ya**
usually implies "and others"; **to** usually implies "and that is all." Thus,
the sentence given under **to**:

### Satō to shio to kome o katta.

砂糖と塩と米を買った。

implies "I bought sugar and salt and rice and nothing more." But the sentence illustrating the use of **ya**, above, implies that besides Tadao and Kiyoshi and Shigeru there were others who went. In English we are usually not aware of this distinction, but it is well if you recognize its existence in Japanese, even though you may not use it yourself.

**kara** is similar to the English preposition *from*, and indicates either space or time: **made** is similar to *until* or *as far as* or *up to*.

> **Koko kara Yokohama made dono kurai desu ka?**
> ここから横浜までどのくらいですか。
> [here from, Yokohama up-to, what amount is *ques* ]
> How far is it from here to Yokohama ?

| | |
|---|---|
| **kore kara** | **sore kara** |
| ここから | それから |
| [this from] | [that from] |
| after this, from now on | after that, and then, next |

| | |
|---|---|
| **kyō made** | **osoku made** |
| 今日まで | 遅くまで |
| [today until] | [late until] |
| until today, up to today | until late |

**ni** can usually be translated as "in" or "to," although it also has many idiomatic uses that may be translated by "at" or "on" or by other English prepositions.

(1) indicating time or location:

> **Densha wa hachi-ji ni demasu.**
> 汽車は八時に出ます。
> [train as-for eight-o'clock at leaves]
> The train leaves at eight.

> **Takusan no otera ga Kyoto ni arimasu.**
> たくさんのお寺が京都にあります。
> [many of *hon*-temples *subj* Kyoto in are]
> There are many temples in Kyoto.

**Kare wa doyōbi ni kimasu.**
彼は土曜日に来ます。
[he as-for Saturday on arrive]
He arrives on Saturday

(2) indicating an indirect object:

**Anata wa Hanako ni tegami o okurimashita ka?**
あなたは花子に手紙を　送りましたか。
[you as-for Hanako to letter *obj* sent *ques*]
Did you send a letter to Hanako?

(3) with verbs meaning "to become" or "to seem":

**Kodomo wa kanai ni nite imasu.**
子どもは家内に似ています。
[child as-for wife to resembling is]
My child takes after my wife.

**Densha de byōki ni narimashita.**
電車で病気になりました。
[train on sick to became]
He became sick on the train.

**e** indicates motion and is equivalent to English *to* or *into*:

**Boku wa asu Tōkyō e ikimasu.**　　**Mori e ikimashō.**
僕はあす東京へ行きます。　　　　森へ行きましょう。
[I as-for tomorrow Tōkyō to go]　　[woods into let's-go]
I shall go to Tōkyō tomorrow.　　　Let's go into the woods.

**de** gathers together several concepts that are not associated in English. It can indicate:

(1) instruments with which things are done; in this sense it is usually translatable as "with" or "by"; this "with" should not be confused with the "with" of accompaniment that is discussed under **to**.

**Enpitsu de kakimashita.**
鉛筆で書きました。
[pencil with wrote]
I wrote with a pencil.

(2) location, usually translated as "at," with verbs other than those meaning "to be":

**Daigaku de Nihongo o benkyō shimashita.**
大学で日本語を勉強しました。
[university at Japanese-language *obj* study did]
I studied Japanese at the university.

(3) Reason or cause, translated as "because of":

**Watashi wa shiken de isogashii.**
私は試験で忙しい。
[I as-for examinations because-of busy]
I am busy because of examinations. I am busy with exams.

**mo** when used alone is equivalent to *also* or *too* or *even*:

**Watashi mo ikimasu.**
私も行きます。
[I too go]
I am going too!

**mo . . . mo**, when used with a positive verb, is equivalent to English *both . . . and*; when used with a negative verb it is equivalent to *neither . . . nor*.

**Kanai mo kodomo mo kaerimasu.**
家内も子どもも帰ります。
[wife both child and return]
Both my wife and child will come back. My wife and child will both come back.

**Kanai mo kodomo mo kaerimasen.**
家内も子どもも帰りません。
[wife both child and not-return]
Neither my wife nor my child will return.


Some of these particles are also used with verbs. In such instances they are equivalent, roughly, to conjunctions in English, and they require a separate discussion (see page 102). The chart on pages 110 through 112 contains all of the particles and postpositions grouped together.*

---

\*  You should also be aware that the words **no** and **de** have other common uses besides as postpositions. **no** (in this usage often abbreviated to **n**) also can be used like the English pronoun *one* ("a big one," "a small one"—but not "one can"). It is also used to turn ordinary clauses into noun clauses or to turn verbs and adjectives into noun constructions. We cover this somewhat difficult idea in more detail on page 88.

> **Kare no kaeru no wa futsū go-ji goro desu.**
> 彼の帰るのは普通五時頃です。
> [he *subj* return fact as-for usually five-o'clock around is]
> As for his returning, it is usually around five o'clock. He usually returns around five o'clock.

> **Akai no o kudasai.**
> 赤いのをください。
> [red one *obj* give]
> Give me a red one.

**de** is often used as if it were a participle of a verb "to be," and in many such instances the material that it governs can be translated into English as a predicate nominative:

> **Boku wa byoki de nete imasu.**
> 僕は病気で寝ています。
> [I as-for sick being in-bed am]
> I am sick and in bed. Since I am sick, I am in bed.

# Words of Demonstration

In Japanese, the demonstrative and interrogative pronouns and adjectives are very closely related in formation to the adverbs that carry similar ideas about place, manner, and sort. All of these words are formed from four basic roots, to which regular endings are added, to form a consistent and logical pattern. We still have remnants of such a pattern in English, where the words *where*, *what*, and *whither* are obviously related to *there*, *that*, and *thither*, but these patterns are developed more widely and more logically in Japanese.

Japanese distinguishes three degrees of distance, just as Spanish and Italian do: (1) near the speaker, corresponding to the English ideas of "here" and "this"; (2) farther removed from the speaker or near the person spoken to, corresponding to "there" and "that"; (3) at a distance from the speaker, not usually differentiated from the second use in English, except by such expressions as "over there," or "that one over there." To these may be added an interrogative mood or a mood of doubt. The basic roots expressing these ideas are:

**ko-** こ [hereness, nearness]
**so-** そ [thereness, not far off, near person addressed]
**a-** あ [thereness, but at a distance]
**do-** ど [question or doubt]

From these roots are made demonstrative pronouns, demonstrative adjectives, phrases of type, adverbs of manner, adverbs of location, adverbs of motion, indefinite pronouns, negative pronouns, and many other forms.

The following endings are added to these roots:

**-re** れ [to indicate a thing]
**-no** の [to indicate demonstrative adjectives]

**-nna** んな [to indicate type of thing, "such a, this kind of . . ."]
vowel lengthening    [manner]
**-ko** こ [location]
**-chira** ちら [direction, motion towards, or preference]


The table below shows how simple this process is.

| | [here] | [there] | [afar] | [question] |
|---|---|---|---|---|
| Root | **ko-**<br>こ | **so-**<br>そ | **a-**<br>あ | **do-**<br>ど |
| Pronouns,<br>**-re** れ | **kore**<br>これ<br>this, this one | **sore**<br>それ<br>that, that one | **are**<br>あれ<br>that, that one | **dore?**<br>どれ<br>which, which one? |
| Adjectives,<br>**-no** の | **kono**<br>この<br>this | **sono**<br>その<br>that | **ano**<br>あの<br>that | **dono?**<br>どの<br>which? |
| Phrase of type<br>**-nna** んな | **konna**<br>こんな<br>this kind of<br>such a | **sonna**<br>そんな<br>that kind of<br>such a | **anna**<br>あんな<br>that kind of<br>such a | **donna ?**<br>どんな<br>what kind of? |
| Mode and<br>manner<br>[vowel<br>lengthening] | **kō**<br>こう<br>like this, so<br>in this way | **sō**<br>そう<br>like that, so<br>in that way | **ā**<br>ああ<br>like that, so<br>in that way | **dō**<br>どう<br>how? in<br>what way? |
| Location<br>**-ko** こ | **Koko**<br>ここ<br>here | **soko**<br>そこ<br>there | **asoko***<br>あそこ<br>there | **doko?**<br>どこ<br>where ? |
| Motion,<br>direction<br>**-chira** ちら | **kochira**<br>こちら<br>here, hither,<br>this | **sochira**<br>そちら<br>there, thith-<br>er, that | **achira**<br>あちら<br>there, thith-<br>er, that | **dochira?**<br>どちら<br>where?<br>which way?<br>which one? |

These words do not change to indicate singular or plural, nor do they have different forms to indicate gender, sex, or the role of the word within the sentence. **kore,** for example, may mean "this," "these," or "them."

---

* Irregularly formed.

When you are referring to persons (except members of your immediate family), it is considered courteous to use combinations of **hito** (meaning "man," "person") or **kata** (meaning "side," with an implication of such respect that a personal pronoun would be improper) with **kono, sono, ano,** and **dono.**

| | |
|---|---|
| **kono hito** or **kono kata** instead of **kare** | he |
| **sono hito** or **sono kata** instead of **sore** | that person, he |
| **ano hito** or **ano kata** instead of **are** | that person at a distance |
| **dono hito** or **dono kata** instead of **dore** | which one |

The forms with **kata** are more courteous than those with **hito.**

**Kono kata ga Suzuki-san desu.**
この方が鈴木さんです。
[this side *subj* Suzuki-Mr. is]
This is Mr. Suzuki.

**Kore ga musume desu.**
これが娘です。
[this *subj* girl is]
This is my daughter.

**sono,** although normally translated as "that," is weaker in feeling as a demonstrative than the English word "that," and very often is simply translated best as "the."

### The Indefinite, Inclusive, and Negative Word Ranges
The interrogative words that have been listed in the table on page 33 are used to form other ranges of meaning: the ideas of "some," of "every," and of "no" or "none." These formations, like those of the demonstrative table, are entirely regular. Particles are added to the interrogative words:

| | | |
|---|---|---|
| **ka** | か | indicates indefiniteness |
| **mo** | も | indicates negation |
| **de mo** | でも | indicates inclusiveness |

The table below shows how these words are formed.

|  | [interrogative] | [indefinite] | [negative] | [distributive] |
|---|---|---|---|---|
| Pronouns for persons | dare?<br>誰?<br>donata?<br>どなた<br>who? | dare ka<br>誰か<br>donata ka<br>どなたか<br>someone | dare mo*<br>誰も<br>donata mo*<br>どなたも<br>no one | dare de mo<br>誰でも<br>donata de mo<br>どなたでも<br>anyone,<br>everyone |
| Pronouns for things and persons | dore?<br>どれ?<br>which? | dore ka<br>どれか<br>something | dore mo*<br>どれも<br>nothing | dore de mo<br>どれでも<br>either one |
| Words of manner | dō<br>どう<br>how? | dō ka<br>どうか<br>somehow | dō mo*<br>どうも<br>not anyhow,<br>in no way | dō de mo<br>どうでも<br>anyhow |
| Words of place | doko?<br>どこ?<br>where? | doko ka<br>どこか<br>somewhere | doko mo*<br>どこも<br>nowhere | doko de mo<br>どこでも<br>anywhere,<br>everywhere |
| Pronouns for things | nani? nan?<br>何?<br>what? | nani ka<br>何か<br>something | nani mo*<br>何も<br>nothing | nan de mo<br>何でも<br>anything,<br>everything |
| Words for direction, preference | dochira<br>どちら<br>where, which | dochira ka<br>どちらか<br>somewhere,<br>one of<br>which | dochira mo*<br>どちらも<br>nowhere,<br>neither of<br>which | dochira de<br>mo<br>どちらでも<br>anywhere,<br>either of<br>which |

Within this table, the **donata** forms are considered to be more courteous than the **dare** forms; **nan** is more colloquial than **nani**. **dochira** indicates "which" in the choice between two objects, while **dore** indicates "which" in the choice among three or more.

---

\* These forms take a negative verb.

# Verbs

## Introduction to Japanese Verbs

This section is a brief anticipation of some of the more important features of the Japanese verb that are likely to be strange to you. We urge you to read this section carefully before you move on to the detailed explanation of verb grammar. It will probably help you to understand some of the unfamiliar constructions and features of form and meaning that must necessarily occur in the sentences that have been quoted as examples.

1. Japanese verbs do not have different forms to indicate the number or person or gender of the subject of the sentence. The same forms are used whether the subject is I or you or they or anything else. Thus the verb form **kaimasu** could mean I buy, you (SING.) buy, he buys, she buys, it buys, we buy, you (PL.) buy, or they buy.

2. Verbs are very often used without a pronoun subject, as in the example above. In such cases you recognize the subject by context. Actually, this is not as difficult as it sounds, and you will very seldom be at a loss about the situation that a verb describes. If there is a question of ambiguity, of course, pronouns may be used.

   You will probably find the Japanese pronounless verbs easier to understand if you remember that the verb in Japanese conveys many aspects of meaning that we think of as belonging to nouns. A translation of the form **kaimasu**, mentioned above, that would catch the spirit of the Japanese form better than our English counterparts, could be simply "act of buying" or "there is an act of buying" or simply "buying."

   Whenever we have given sentences in which the verb is not accompanied by a subject pronoun, we have supplied the English translation with the subject pronoun that a conversational context might require. In most cases, however, other pronouns could fit into a translation equally well. Where we have translated "I," you could read with equal reason "you" or "he" or "they" or another personal pronoun. (See page 119, the section on honorific forms, however, for instances where the verb forms or other words definitely restrict the meaning to one pronoun-idea.)

3. There are only two real tenses in Japanese, a present and a past. Japanese is not so much interested in the subtleties of time as is English or some of the other Indo-European languages. There is no true future tense; the present is used to express definite future ideas:

**Tōkyō e ikimashita.** (PAST TENSE)
東京へ行きました。
[Tōkyō to went]
I went to Tōkyō.

**Tōkyō e ikimasu.** (PRESENT TENSE)
東京へ行きます。
[Tōkyō to go]
I go to Tōkyō. I shall go to Tōkyō.

4. Although tenses are few, Japanese is extremely rich in verb forms that indicate moods or aspects of likeness, or belief on the part of the speaker, or appearances. Most of these are beyond the scope of this manual, but there is one such mood that is important and must be learned. This is a form that is called the probable mood. It indicates that action will probably occur, is probably occurring, may occur, etc. We have described it in more detail on page 48. **kaeru deshō**, for example, might be translated "he is probably returning," "he will probably return," "I think he will return," and so on.

5. There are several compound verb forms that are frequently used. There is a progressive aspect that corresponds surprisingly closely to the English form in meaning and formation (see page 46). It is made with a participle and a conjugated form of a verb meaning "to be."

**Nani o shite imasu ka?**
何をしていますか。
[what *obj* doing is *ques*]
What is he doing?

6. Each Japanese verb has an entire negative conjugation to balance

its possible forms. Unlike English, where you simply add *no* or *not* to most sentences to make a negative, Japanese has completely different verb forms to indicate a negative idea. If you wanted to say, "I bought a book," you would say either:

ABRUPT

**Hon o katta.**
本を買った。
[book *obj* bought]
I bought a book.

or

POLITE

**Hon o kaimashita.**
本を買いました。
[book *obj* bought]
I bought a book.

To say, "I did not buy a book," you would have to say:

ABRUPT

**Hon o kawanakatta.**
本を買わなかった。
[book *obj* not-bought]
I did not buy a book.

or

POLITE

**Hon o kaimasen deshita.**
本を買いませんでした。
[book *obj* not-buy was]
I did not buy a book.

7. You will observe that two versions of the same idea have been given in the sentence above. Each verb has two sets of forms: (a) its true forms made by conjugating the verb itself (the forms on the left), and (b) courtesy forms that are made by using a stem of the verb, and adding to it various forms of an ending whose stem is -**mas**-. (See page 114 for a complete conjugation.) The feeling of the language, in general, is that the true conjugational forms are too abrupt for polite usage in many places within the sentence, and that the politer forms in -**mas**- must be substituted. (This is not a complete statement of the uses of the polite and abrupt forms, but simply an advance hint. The subject is dealt with in detail in the following pages.)

8. Japanese verbs are highly regular. There are only two really irregular verbs in the language, and these are irregular only in their stems. There are perhaps a half dozen other common verbs that are very slightly irregular in one or two forms. As a result, even though there are more forms per verb than there are in English, and the endings used to make particular forms are longer than English endings, the Japanese verb is really very simple. Verbs are so completely regular in the way they make their forms that you will be astonished at the ease with which you will master them.

## Verb Conjugations and the Basic Stem

All Japanese verbs (with the exception of two irregular verbs, **suru**, "to do," and **kuru**, "to come") can be classified, according to the way they make their forms, into two major groupings or conjugations. These conjugations are usually called (1) the consonant conjugation (or the **u**-conjugation or the **u**-dropping conjugation) and (2) the vowel conjugation (or the **ru**-conjugation, or the **ru**-dropping conjugation). The two conjugations differ only in the way that they form their basic and secondary stems; otherwise, they are identical.

### The Consonant or *U*-dropping Conjugation

Most of the verbs in this conjugation are easy to recognize. If the end syllables of the dictionary form of a verb are anything at all but -**eru** or -**iru**, the verb is automatically a member of the **u**-dropping conjugation. The possible endings are:

**-bu -mu -nu -ku -gu -su -tsu**
**-au -iu -ou -aru -oru -uru**[*]

All of these verbs form their basic stem by dropping the final -**u** and making whatever phonetic changes are necessary :[†]

| PRESENT FORM | | | BASIC STEM |
|---|---|---|---|
| **tobu** | 飛ぶ | to fly | **tob-** |
| **yomu** | 読む | to read | **yom-** |
| **shinu** | 死ぬ | to die | **shin-** |
| **kaku** | 書く | to write | **kak-** |
| **isogu** | 急ぐ | to hurry | **isog-** |
| **dasu** | 出す | to take out, to present | **das-** |
| **matsu** | 待つ | to wait | **mat-** |
| **shimau** | しまう | to finish | **shima-**[‡] |
| **kau** | 買う | to buy | **ka-**[‡] |
| **iu** | 言う | to say | **i-**[‡] |
| **omou** | 思う | to think | **omo-**[‡] |
| **aru** | ある | to be, to have | **ar-** |
| **toru** | 取る | to take | **tor-** |
| **nuru** | 塗る | to paint | **nur-** |

---

[*]   All Japanese verbs end (in their dictionary or present form) in the letter -**u**.
[†]   See pages 138 ff.
[‡]   Strictly speaking these stems end in a -**w**-; for convenient exposition we can ignore this -**w**-.

Observe that the stem of **matsu** is not **mats-**, but **mat-**. This results from a peculiarity of the Japanese phonemic system: the phonetic combination -**tu**, which would be expected for the dictionary form, is not possible in Japanese; its place is taken by the phonetic combination -**tsu**. The table of kana in the appendix to this manual lists other combinations of letters which are not possible in Japanese.

If the final syllables of a verb are -**eru** or -**iru**, however, it is not possible to tell from the present form to which conjugation a verb belongs.* A few verbs ending in -**eru** and -**iru** are members of the **u**-dropping conjugation, and form their basic stem (like other members of the conjugation) by dropping the final -**u**:

| PRESENT FORM | | | BASIC STEM |
|---|---|---|---|
| **shiru** | 知る | to know | **shir-** |
| **hairu** | 入る | to enter | **hair-** |
| **kaeru** | 帰る | to return | **kaer-** |

### The Vowel or *Ru*-dropping Conjugation

Most verbs ending in -**eru** or -**iru**, however, are members of the second, or **ru**-dropping conjugation. They form their basic stem by dropping -**ru**:

| PRESENT FORM | | | BASIC STEM |
|---|---|---|---|
| **dekiru** | できる | to be able | **deki-** |
| **iru** | いる | to be | **i-** |
| **hajimeru** | 始める | to begin | **hajime-** |
| **kangaeru** | 考える | to think | **kangae-** |
| **taberu** | 食べる | to eat | **tabe-** |
| **ageru** | あげる | to raise, to give | **age-** |
| **miru** | 見る | to see | **mi-** |

In both conjugations the basic stem gives rise to all other verb forms in an entirely regular manner. For this reason it is very important that you understand how to isolate it.

---

* For example, the word **kiru** (stress on **KI**), meaning "to cut," belongs to the **u**-dropping conjugation, and its stem is **kir-**. **kiru** (stress on the **RU**), meaning "to wear," belongs to the **ru**-dropping conjugation and its stem is **ki-**. This confusion occurs, however, only when the words are spelled in the romaji, or Latin, alphabet or in kana, the Japanese syllabary. If the character for the word is used, there is, of course, no possibility of confusion.

## The Combining Stem and the Polite Forms

The most important secondary stem for the beginner in Japanese is the so-called combining stem (also called the conjunctive stem, indefinite base, main stem, or second base). It serves as the base (1) for forming the polite forms that end most sentences, (2) for expressing wishes, (3) for making various special constructions, and (in some cases) (4) for creating a verbal noun. It is indispensable to even the most elementary knowledge of Japanese.

The combining stem is formed from the basic stem by adding -i- to the basic stem of **u**-dropping verbs and by adding nothing to the basic stem of **ru**-dropping verbs.

### u-dropping verbs

| PRESENT FORM | | | BASIC STEM | COMBINING STEM |
|---|---|---|---|---|
| **iru** | 要る | to need | **ir-** | **iri-** |
| **dasu** | 出す | to take out | **das-** | **dashi-** |
| **motsu** | 持つ | to hold | **mot-** | **mochi-** |
| **yomu** | 読む | to read | **yom-** | **yomi-** |

### ru-dropping verbs

| | | | | |
|---|---|---|---|---|
| **taberu** | 食べる | to eat | **tabe-** | **tabe-** |
| **kiru** | 着る | to wear | **ki-** | **ki-** |

Observe the phonetic changes in the verbs **dasu** and **motsu**.*

The entire range of polite forms is made from this combining stem. Since it is felt that the true final forms of a verb (see page 114) are too abrupt for use (in most circumstances) at the end of a sentence, almost every Japanese sentence that you will hear will probably end in one of these polite forms. They are made by adding the following suffixes to the combining stem of all verbs:

| | POSITIVE | | NEGATIVE | |
|---|---|---|---|---|
| Present | **-masu** | ます | **-masen** | ません |
| Past | **-mashita** | ました | **-masen deshita** | ませんでした |
| Probable | **-mashō** | ましょう | **-masen deshō** | ませんでしょう |

---

* See pages 138 ff.

While there are other polite forms in the -**mas**- group, these are the most common, and the ones that you will find indispensable. With these six forms you should be able to express almost any verb idea that is likely to be necessary, if you avoid complex sentences, relative constructions, and other expressions that are not simple.

> **Watashi wa ikimasu.** (**iku** "to go," combining stem, **iki**-)
> 私は行きます。
> [I as-for go]
> I shall go. I go.

> **Watashi wa ikimasen.**
> 私は行きません。
> [I as-for go-not]
> I shall not go. I do not go.

All verbs are regular in the formation of these polite forms, although the two irregular verbs **suru** (to do) and **kuru** (to come) have irregular combining stems:

| PRESENT FORM | COMBINING STEM | POLITE FORM |
|---|---|---|
| **kuru** 来る to come | **ki**- | **kimasu** 来ます |
| **suru** する to do | **shi**- | **shimasu** しません |

Five other verbs are slightly irregular in dropping an -**r**- when they make their combining stems:

| PRESENT FORM | COMBINING STEM | POLITE FORM |
|---|---|---|
| **gozaru**<br>ござる<br>to be<br>[formal, polite] | **gozai**- | **gozaimasu**<br>ございます |
| **irassharu**<br>いらしゃる<br>to go, to be, to come<br>[very formal, polite] | **irasshai**- | **irasshaimasu**<br>いらっしゃいます |

| PRESENT FORM | COMBINING STEM | POLITE FORM |
|---|---|---|
| **kudasaru** | **kudasai-** | **kudasaimasu** |
| くださる | | くださいます |
| to give | | |
| [polite, formal] | | |
| | | |
| **nasaru** | **nasai-** | **nasaimasu** |
| なさる | | なさいます |
| to do | | |
| [polite, formal] | | |
| | | |
| **ossharu** | **osshai-** | **osshaimasu** |
| おっしゃる | | おっしゃいます |
| to say | | |
| [very formal, polite] | | |

These five verbs are extremely important, and their polite forms are indispensable to ordinary polite discourse. We shall discuss the politeness-function of these five verbs in a later section on special courtesy forms.

**Sensei ga sore o nasaimasu.**
先生がそれをなさいます。
[teacher *subj* that *obj* does]
The teacher is doing it.

**Anokata wa shichō-san de gozaimasu.**
あの方は市長さんでございます。
[that-person as-for mayor — is]
That person over there is the mayor.

**Yamada-san wa irasshaimasu ka?**
山田さんはいらっしゃいますか。
[Yamada-Mr. as-for is *ques*]
Is Mr. Yamada here?

**Koko ni seikyūsho ga gozaimasu.**
ここに請求書がございます。
[here in bill (or check) *subj* is]
Here is a bill (or check).

**Sensei ga irasshaimasu.**
先生がいらっしゃいます。
[teacher *subj* comes]
The teacher comes. The teacher will come.

## The Present

The verb form that is given in the dictionary is called the present or the present final. It always ends in -**u**.

Basically, its meaning is that of the English present, although it is also used to express future time, since Japanese has no separate future tense. It does not change to show the person or number of the subject, but remains unaltered. Thus, **kaeru** (to return) may, according to context, mean: I return, you (SING.) return, he returns, we return, you (PL.) return, they return, I shall return, you (SING.) will return, he will return, we shall return, you (PL.) will return, they will return.

**Gakusei wa hon o kau.**
学生は本を買う。
[students as-for books *obj* buy]
The students buy books.

**Tomodachi ni tegami o kaku.**
友達に手紙を書く。
[friend to letters *obj* write]
He writes letters to his friend.

**Ashita Ueno no sakura o mi ni iku.**
あした上野の桜を見に行く。
[tomorrow Ueno of cherry blossom *obj* see in-order-to go]
Tomorrow I shall go to see the cherry blossoms at Ueno.

This form is felt to be somewhat abrupt, though, and in usual polite conversation it will be replaced at sentence ends with the polite forms that have already been covered (see page 39). The above sentences would then read, with no change of meaning beyond increased courtesy:

**Gakusei wa hon o kaimasu.**
学生は本を買います。

**Tomodachi ni tegami o kakimasu.**
友達に手紙を書きます。

**Ashita Ueno no sakura o mi ni ikimasu.**
あした上野の桜を見に行きます。

The present final form is still used, nevertheless, in two other places within the body of the sentence: (1) in dependent clauses, with certain conjunctions (see page 102); and (2) within relative constructions (see page 86 for a discussion of this highly idiomatic construction).

**Hima ga *aru* toki, shōsetsu o yomimasu.**
ひまがある時、小説を読みます。
[free-time *subj* is when, novels *obj* read]
When I have the time, I read novels.

**Boku no Nihon ni *iru* tomodachi wa Kanazawa to *iu* machi ni sunde imasu.**
僕の日本にいる友達は金沢と言う町に住んでいます。
[I of Japan in is friend as-for Kanazawa thus call city in living is]
My friend who is in Japan is living in a city called Kanazawa.

## The Past

The past tense (or past final or simple past tense) is used to express events that took place in the past, and is roughly equivalent to the English past (I walked) and present perfect (I have walked).

It is entirely regular in formation, except for the two irregular verbs **kuru** (to come) and **suru** (to do).

To make the past tense of a verb in the vowel (or **ru**-dropping) conjugation, you simply add -**ta** to the basic stem:

| PRESENT FORM | | | BASIC STEM | PAST FORM | | |
|---|---|---|---|---|---|---|
| **miru** | 見る | to see | **mi-** | **mita** | 見た | saw |
| **oshieru** | 教える | to teach | **oshie-** | **oshieta** | 教えた | taught |
| **akeru** | 開ける | to open | **ake-** | **aketa** | 開けた | opened |
| **shimeru** | 閉める | to close | **shime-** | **shimeta** | 閉めた | closed |

In the consonant conjugation (or **u**-dropping conjugation), however, the situation is not so simple. Sound changes are made in certain syllables, according to the final consonant of the basic stem. These changes are entirely regular, but the rules are complex, and it will be probably easier for you simply to memorize the changes, without bothering with the rules of juncture that produce them.

| STEMS ENDING IN | FORM THE PAST BY SUBSTITUTING | PRESENT FORM | PAST FORM |
|---|---|---|---|
| **-ku** く | **-ita** | **kaku**<br>書く<br>to write | **kaita**<br>書いた<br>wrote |
| **-gu** ぐ | **-ida** | **isogu**<br>急ぐ<br>to hurry | **isoida**<br>急いだ<br>hurried |
| **-tsu** つ | **-tta** | **matsu**<br>待つ<br>to wait | **matta**<br>待った<br>waited |
| **-ru** る | **-tta** | **toru**<br>取る<br>to take | **totta**<br>取った<br>took |
| vowel | **-tta** | **au**<br>会う<br>to meet | **atta**<br>会った<br>met |
| plus **-u** う | | **omou**<br>思う<br>to think | **omotta**<br>思った<br>thought |
| | | **iu**<br>言う<br>to say | **itta**<br>言った<br>said |
| **-mu** む | **-nda** | **yomu**<br>読む<br>to read | **yonda**<br>読んだ<br>read |
| **-nu** ぬ | **-nda** | **shinu**<br>死ぬ<br>to die | **shinda**<br>死んだ<br>died |
| **-bu** ぶ | **-nda** | **yobu**<br>呼ぶ<br>to call | **yonda**<br>呼んだ<br>called |
| **-su** す | **-shita** | **hanasu**<br>話す<br>to speak | **hanashita**<br>話した<br>spoke |

Notice that verbs ending in -**tsu**, -**ru**, and vowel + **u** all form their past in the same way—by changing the final syllable to -**tta**; and verbs ending in -**mu**, -**nu**, -**bu** all change the final syllable to -**nda**. As a result, verbs like **yobu** and **yomu** will both have the same past form, **yonda**, as will **au** and **aru**, **atta**. You must determine which meaning is intended by context.

The following two forms are irregular:

| PRESENT FORM | | | PAST FORM | | |
|---|---|---|---|---|---|
| **kuru** | 来る | to come | **kita** | 来た | came |
| **suru** | する | to do, make | **shita** | した | made, did |

The past tense is used in the same situations within the sentence as is the present. (1) It may be used at the end of a sentence, but it is felt to be somewhat abrupt, hence its place is taken in ordinary polite conversation by the corresponding polite form, which is made by adding -**mashita** to the combining stem (see page 39). (2) It is the form usually used within relative clauses (see page 86). (3) It is sometimes used before certain conjunctions, although the polite form ending in -**mashita** may also be used here (see page 102).

**Watashi wa shigoto ga atta no de kaerimashita.**
私は仕事があったので帰りました。
[I as-for job *subj* was because of returned]
I returned because there was a job to do. I returned because I had something to do.

**Mado o aketa.**
窓を開けた。
[window *obj* opened]
I opened the window.

## The Participle

One of the most useful forms in Japanese is the participle. As we shall demonstrate in the following sections, it is used to form the progressive tenses (see page 46), polite commands (page 52), perfected action (see pages 47–48), suspending forms of verbs (see pages 84 ff.), and many idiomatic constructions.

All participles are completely regular: they are formed by changing the -**a** of the past to -**e**:

| PRESENT FORM | PAST FORM | PARTICIPLE |
|---|---|---|
| **taberu** | **tabeta** | **tabete** |
| 食べる | 食べた | 食べて |
| to eat | ate | eating |
| **kuru** | **kita** | **kite** |
| 来る | 来た | 来て |
| to come | came | coming |
| **suru** | **shita** | **shite** |
| する | した | して |
| to do | did | doing |
| **kaeru** | **kaetta** | **kaette** |
| 帰る | 帰った | 帰って |
| to return | returned | returning |
| **iru** | **ita** | **ite** |
| いる | いた | いて |
| to be | was | being |
| **kaku** | **kaita** | **kaite** |
| 来る | 来た | 来て |
| to write | wrote | writing |
| **yomu** | **yonda** | **yonde** |
| 読む | 読んだ | 読んで |
| to read | read | reading |

We have translated these forms as English present participles, but it must be remembered that in Japanese these forms are entirely verbal in meaning. They cannot be used as nouns, as we sometimes use the present participle, nor can they be used as adjectives. Such sentences as "Eating is the greatest of pleasures" or "Coming events cast their shadows before them" cannot be translated literally into Japanese.

## Progressive Tenses
Japanese, like English, has a range of progressive tenses that are indispensable to ordinary conversation. Indicating action that is contin-

ued over a period of time, they are formed (very much as in English) by using the participle (see page 45) and an appropriate form of the auxiliary verb **iru** (to be). The forms of **iru** which you will normally encounter in this construction are **iru** (present), **ita** (past), **irō** or **iru darō** (probable), or their more polite counterparts **imasu** (present), **imashita** (past), **imasho** or **iru deshō** (probable).

NORMAL                                  MORE COURTEOUS

**suru** する to do

| NORMAL | MORE COURTEOUS |
|---|---|
| **Kare wa nani o shite iru ka?** | **Kare wa nani o shite imasu ka?** |
| 彼は何をしているか。 | 彼は何をしていますか。 |
| [he as-for what *obj* doing is *ques*] | [he as-for what *obj* doing is *ques*] |
| What is he doing? | What is he doing? |

**naosu** 直す to mend, repair

| | |
|---|---|
| **Kare wa kyāburētā o naoshite ita.** | **Kare wa kyāburētā o naoshite imashita.** |
| 彼はキャブレーターを直していた。 | 彼はキャブレーターを直していました。 |
| [he as-for carburetor *obj* repairing was] | [he as-for carburetor repairing was] |
| He was repairing the carburetor. | He was repairing the carburetor. |

**matsu** 待つ to wait

| | |
|---|---|
| **Boku no kaeri o matte iru.** | **Boku no kaeri o matte imashō.** |
| 僕の帰りを待っているだろう。 | 僕の帰りを待っていましょう |
| [I of return *obj* waiting may-be] | [I of return *obj* waiting may-be] |
| They are probably waiting for me. | They are probably waiting for me. |

On the whole, the Japanese and English uses of progressive tenses correspond, although there are two differences of some importance. (1) Japanese does not use progressive tenses to indicate future time, as we do. We say, "Tomorrow I am going. . . ." Japanese cannot say this, but must say, "Tomorrow we go. . . ." (2) Japanese often uses a progressive form where we would use a simple form. In instances where an action has lasted from the past into the present, for us the progressive meaning has just about disappeared, although Japanese still considers these ideas durational:

**kawaku** 乾く to dry (intransitive)

**Sentakumono wa kawaite imasu.**
洗濯物は乾いています。
[laundry as-for drying is]
The laundry is dry.

This idiomatic usage is ordinarily found with intransitive verbs. You need not use it yourself, since it is difficult to apply correctly, but you should be able to recognize it if you hear it.

Verbs that mean "knowing" or "thinking" are often used in a progressive form, even though we would use a simple tense in English:

**oboeru** 覚える to remember

**Ano kata no namae o oboete imasu ka?**
あの方の名前を覚えていますか。
[he of name *obj* remembering are *ques*]
Do you remember that man's name ?

**shiru** 知る to know

**Kotae o shitte imasu ka?**
答えを知っていますか。
[answer *obj* knowing is *ques*]
Do you know the answer?

## The Probable Mood

Japanese has a special mood that is used to indicate possibility, probability, belief, doubt, and similar concepts that exist around the boundary lines of what has actually taken place. This mood, which has no exact counterpart in English, is used very frequently in Japanese, and you must be able to use at least the present form of it.

Japanese is extremely rich in forms that show the speaker's relationship to what he is saying—whether he gives it full credence, whether he is in doubt, and so on—and there are several different ways of forming the probable mood. There are slight shades of meaning between the different forms, though these shades are too subtle for correct usage by English speakers, too difficult to formulate clearly, and in any case beyond the scope of this manual. We shall indicate only basic situations.

Each verb has a true conjugational form for the probable mood. The consonant conjugation (**u**-dropping conjugation) changes the final -**u** of the present form to -**ō**:

| PRESENT | | PROBABLE | |
|---|---|---|---|
| **iku** 行く to go | | **ikō** 行こう | I will probably go |
| **nomu** 飲む to drink | | **nomō** 飲もう | I will probably drink |

The vowel conjugation (**ru**-dropping conjugation) adds the syllable -**yō** to the basic stem:

| PRESENT | BASIC STEM | PROBABLE |
|---|---|---|
| **kariru** 借りる to rent | **kari-** | **kariyō** 借りよう |
| **taberu** 食べる to eat | **tabe-** | **tabeyō** 食べよう |

The irregular verbs **kuru** (to come) and **suru** (to do) have, respectively, the forms **koyō** and **shiyō**.

You should be aware of two important concepts covered by this form: (1) a probable mood where there is a strong feeling of doubt:

**Ame ga furō ga kamaimasen.**
雨が降ろうがかまいません。
[rain *subj* would-fall although, not-matter]
Even if it did rain, it would not matter.

and (2) an indication of determination or exhortation. In this use the probable can be only in the present tense, and must apply to a first-person subject (I or we):

| **Ikō!** | **Boku ga ikō.** |
|---|---|
| 行こう | 僕が行こう |
| [would-go] | [I *subj* would-go] |
| Let us go! | I will go. (with a strong feeling of determination) |

As is the case with many other true conjugational forms of a verb, these probable forms of the verb are abrupt in some situations, and in normal polite discourse their place is taken by forms ending in

-**mashō** (which is related to the -**masu** and -**mashita** you have already learned). -**mashō** is added to the combining stem of the verb:

| PRESENT | COMBINING STEM | NORMAL POLITE PROBABLE |
|---|---|---|
| **iku** or **yuku** | **iki-** or **yuki-** | **ikimashō** or **yukimashō** |
| 行く | | 行きましょう |
| to go | | |
| **taberu** | **tabe-** | **tabemashō** |
| 食べる | | 食べましょう |
| to eat | | |
| **nomu** | **nomi-** | **nomimashō** |
| 飲む | | 飲みましょう |
| to drink | | |

| | |
|---|---|
| **Ikimashō!** | **Ippai nomimashō.** |
| 行きましょう | 一杯飲みましょう。 |
| [would-go] | [one-cup would-drink] |
| Let's go! Let us go! | Let us drink one cup. |

The second important form of the probable mood is made by placing the verb form **darō** after the present tense of the verb you wish to use:

PRESENT
**iku**    行く    to go    **iku darō**    行くだろう    will probably go
**kariru** 借りる to rent **kariru darō** 借りるだろう will probably rent

This form is somewhat abrupt, and in normal polite conversation its place is taken by the present plus **deshō**:

**iku deshō**    行くでしょう    would probably go
**kariru deshō** 借りるでしょう would probably rent

This form conveys a stronger idea of probability than the conjugational form **ikō** or its polite equivalent **ikimasho**. In questions it often can be translated with the flavor of "Is it probable that . . . ," "Do you think that . . . ." Since Japanese has no true future forms, and the future is at once indeterminate and probable, the probable forms are often translatable by an English future tense.

**Kare wa kuru deshō ka?**

彼は来るでしょうか。

[he as-for come probably *ques*]

Do you think he will come? I wonder if he will come?

**Ame ga furu deshō ga kamaimasen.**

雨が降るでしょうがかまいません。

[rain *subj* fall probably but does-not-matter]

It will probably rain, but it does not matter. I think it will rain, but it
    does not matter.

This probable form with **darō** or **deshō** can be used in the past
tense and in negative forms:

**nomu** 飲む to drink

PRESENT

| POSITIVE | NEGATIVE |
|---|---|
| **nomu darō** | **nomanai darō** |
| 飲むだろう | 飲まないだろう |
| **nomu deshō** | **nomanai deshō** |
| 飲むでしょう | 飲まないでしょう |
| would probably drink | would probably not drink |

PAST

| | |
|---|---|
| **nonda darō** | **nomanakatta darō** |
| 飲んだだろう | 飲まなかっただろう |
| **nonda deshō** | **nomanakatta deshō** |
| 飲んだでしょう | 飲まなかったでしょう |
| probably drank | probably did not drink |

As you may have observed, these forms are simply the normal past
forms and the normal negative forms of the verb, to which are added
**darō** or **deshō**.

Do not be too discouraged if you are doubtful when you should use
the **ikō**, **ikimashō** forms and when the **iku darō**, **iku deshō** forms.
It is sufficient if you recognize them as probables. If you use them
somewhat incorrectly, you will probably still be understood.

## Commands

Japanese has true command forms (or imperatives), but they are felt to be very abrupt, even discourteous. The chances are that you will not encounter them. Instead, you will probably hear commands and requests expressed in other ways. Two of these ways you should learn, since they will be indispensable to you.

In ordinary polite speech the most common way of expressing a command or request is by means of the word **kudasai** (by derivation, "give" or "grant" or "condescend to"). **kudasai**, which does not change in form, is used as the final verb form, and the word that indicates the desired action is used in the participle form directly before **kudasai**.

**akeru** 開ける to open    **akete** 開けて opening

**Mado o akete kudasai.**
窓を開けてください。
[window *obj* opening please]
Please open the window.

The word **dōzo** "please" is very often used as the first word of the sentence to make the request even more polite:

**shimeru** 閉める to close    **shimete** 閉めて closing

**Dōzo to o shimete kudasai.**
どうぞ戸を閉めてください。
[please door *obj* closing please]
Please close the door.

When you request an object, **kudasai** is used with its proper meaning of "give," and takes a normal direct object:

**Ocha o kudasai.**
お茶をください。
[tea *obj* give]
Please give me some tea.

**kudasai** is the normal way in which you will make a request or utter a command if the feeling of the situation is that of asking a favor. The way to order something to be done is with the form **nasai**, which is less polite than **kudasai**, but nevertheless more polite than true imperatives. **nasai** is attached to the combining stem of the verb; **dōzo** would not be used with it.

| **Mado o akenasai.** | **To o shimenasai.** |
|---|---|
| 窓を開けなさい。 | 戸を閉めなさい。 |
| [window *obj* opening do] | [door *obj* closing do] |
| Open the window, please. | Please close the door. |

Negative commands and prohibitions are not so easy to form. For **kudasai**, you would use the negative participle form of the verb (explained on page 55) and **kudasai**. This negative form ends in -**naide**:

**kamau** 構う to bother   **kamawanaide** 構わないで not bothering

**Kamawanaide kudasai.**
構わないでください。
[not-bothering please]
Don't bother, please. Don't trouble yourself.

## Negative Verbs

Japanese expresses negative sentences in a different way than English does. Instead of using words like *no* or *not* to change the meaning of the sentence from positive to negative, Japanese has a separate negative conjugation, which parallels all the forms of the ordinary positive conjugation of the verb.

We have already given hints of this situation in the section on polite forms (page 39), where it was stated that -**masu** is a polite termination for a positive verb in the present tense, while -**masen** is its negative counterpart. Besides these polite forms, -**masen** and -**masen deshita**, each verb also has its own proper conjugational forms, which are abrupt in meaning. These true negative forms are built upon a different stem than the polite negatives, and you must be careful not to confuse the two stems.

These true negative forms are extremely important in Japanese, and complex though they may seem, you should be able to understand them. Learn the forms first; we shall discuss their use later.

The abrupt negative conjugation is built upon the basic stem of the verb. Verbs of the consonant (**u**-dropping) conjugation add -**a**- to the basic stem to form a negative stem:

| PRESENT | | BASIC STEM | NEGATIVE STEM |
|---|---|---|---|
| **kaku** 書く | to write | **kak-** | **kaka-** |
| **hairu** 入る | to enter | **hair-** | **haira-** |
| **kau** 買う | to buy | **ka-** | **kawa-**\* |
| **iu** 言う | to say | **i-** | **iwa-**\* |

Verbs of the vowel (**ru**-dropping) conjugation use the same form for basic stem and negative stem:

| PRESENT | | BASIC STEM | NEGATIVE STEM |
|---|---|---|---|
| **ochiru** 落ちる | to fall | **ochi-** | **ochi-** |
| **wasureru** 忘れる | to forget | **wasure-** | **wasure-** |

Negative forms are then made by adding the appropriate form of the adjective -**nai** to the negative stem for both conjugations of verbs.

| PRESENT | BASIC STEM | NEGATIVE STEM | NEGATIVE |
|---|---|---|---|
| **kaku**<br>書く<br>to write | **kak-** | **kaka-** | **kakanai**<br>書かない<br>I do not write |
| **hairu**<br>入る<br>to enter | **hair-** | **haira-** | **hairanai**<br>入らない<br>I do not enter |
| **kau**<br>買う<br>to buy | **ka-** | **kawa-** | **kawanai**<br>買わない<br>I do not buy |
| **iu**<br>言う<br>to say | **i-** | **iwa-** | **iwanai**<br>言わない<br>I do not say |
| **ochiru**<br>落ちる<br>to fall | **ochi-** | **ochi-** | **ochinai**<br>落ちない<br>I do not fall |
| **wasureru**<br>忘れる<br>to forget | **wasure-** | **wasure-** | **wasurenai**<br>忘れない<br>I do not forget |

---

\*   Verbs ending in -**ou**, -**iu**, -**au** are considered historically to have a -**w**- phoneme within the vowel combination; this emerges in the negative stem.

Negative forms of the progressive tenses are made by using the ordinary positive participle, plus negative forms of the verb **iru** (or its polite equivalents). **iru**, as you will observe, takes the same -**nai** endings as other verbs (**iru**, "to be," **ru**-dropping conjugation, negative stem **i**-, combining stem **i**-):

## kaku 書く to write

|  | ABRUPT | POLITE | |
|---|---|---|---|
| Present | **kaite inai**<br>書いていない | **kaite imasen**<br>書いていません | is not writing |
| Past | **kaite inakatta**<br>書いてなかった | **kaite imasen deshita**<br>書いていませんでした | was not writing |
| Probable | **kaite inakarō**<br>書いていなかろう<br>(or **kaite inai darō**)<br>書いていないだろう | **kaite imasen deshō**<br>書いていませんでしょう<br>(or **kaite inai deshō**)<br>書いていないでしょう | is probably not<br>writing |

All verbs are regular in the negative conjugation with the following exceptions:

| | | | | | |
|---|---|---|---|---|---|
| **suru** | する | to do | **shinai**, etc. しない | is not doing |
| **kuru** | 来る | to come | **konai**, etc. 来ない | is not coming |
| **aru** | ある | to be | **nai**, etc. ない | is not being |

As has been the case with other conjugational verb forms, the true negative forms are felt to be somewhat abrupt, and in polite conversation you should use their polite equivalents at the end of a sentence (see table, p. 56). Observe that the polite forms do not use the negative stem, but the combining stem.

### Verbs Conjugated with *suru*

Japanese has borrowed an enormous number of words from Chinese, just as English has from French and Latin. These Chinese-Japanese words are usually the words of the Buddhist religion, of literature, of science, of high courtesy, of culture, and of abstract thought, just as Romance words usually express similar ideas in English. Some of these words are indispensable to daily life.

## Negative Forms of the Verb

| kiku 聞く to hear | | | |
|---|---|---|---|
| | FORMS OF **NAI** | ABRUPT NEGATIVE | POLITE NEGATIVE |
| Present | -nai<br>ない | kikanai<br>聞かない | kikimasen<br>聞きません<br>does not hear |
| Past | -nakatta<br>なかった | kikanakatta<br>聞かなかった | kikimasen deshita<br>聞きませんでした<br>did not hear |
| Probable | -nakarō<br>なかろう | kikanakaro<br>聞かなかろう<br>or kikanai daro<br>聞かないだろう | kikimasen deshō<br>聞きませんでしょう<br>or kikanai deshō<br>聞かないでしょう<br>probably does not hear |
| Present cond.* | -nakereba<br>なければ | kikanakereba<br>聞かなければ | — —<br>if I don't hear |
| Past cond.* | -nakattara<br>なかったら | kikanakattara<br>聞かなかったら | — —<br>if I didn't hear |
| Participle | -nakute<br>なくて<br>-naide<br>ないで | kikanakute<br>聞かなくて<br>kikanaide<br>聞かないで | — —<br>not hearing |

Unlike native Japanese verbs, which we have discussed up to now, these verbs of Chinese origin do not make their own forms; they remain unchanged. Instead, they are conjugated by adding to them appropriate forms of the auxiliary verb **suru**, "to do" or "to make." As you will see, the idea behind this formation is not very different from that of such English expressions as *to make ready, to do justice to, to do penance, to make do,* and so on.

You will find thousands of these Chinese verb roots in your dictionary. Sometimes they are presented with the verb **suru** in full: **ai suru** (to love); sometimes they are represented by an abbreviation: **ai s.**

---

\* For recognition only.

The following forms are typical:

| chūi suru 注意する to pay attention | | |
|---|---|---|
| | NORMAL OR ABRUPT FORMS | POLITE FORMS |
| Present | chūi suru 注意する | chūi shimasu 注意します |
| Past | chūi shita 注意した | chūi shimashita 注意しました |
| Probable | chūi suru darō 注意するだろう | chūi shimashō 注意しましょう or chūi suru deshō 注意するでしょう |
| Participle | chūi shite 注意して | |
| Present negative | chūi shinai 注意しない | chūi shimasen 注意しません |
| Past negative | chūi shinakatta 注意しなかった | chūi shimasen deshita 注意しませんでした |
| Probable negative | chūi shinakarō 注意しなかろう or chūi shinai darō 注意しないだろう | chūi shimasen deshō 注意しませんでしょう or chūi shinai deshō 注意しないでしょう |
| Neg. participle | chūi shinakute 注意しなくて | chūi shinaide 注意しないで |
| Present progressive | chūi shite iru 注意している | chūi shite imasu, etc. 注意しています |
| Present progressive negative | chūi shite inai 注意していない | chūi shite imasen, etc. 注意していません |

All of these tenses and forms are made according to the conjugation of **suru**, which is regular except for its stems.

### The Verb "to be"
In English we express quite a few different ideas by means of the single verb "to be." We use to it to mean "is located," "has the characteristic of," "equals," and "is engaged in the activity of." Japanese uses different

words to express these different ideas. It is very important that you master them, or your Japanese is likely to be unintelligible. We shall tabulate these verbs first, then discuss them in some detail:

| VERB | MEANING | HOW USED |
|---|---|---|
| **iru** いる | to be located | used with living beings |
| ——— | | auxiliary to form the progressive |
| **aru** ある | to be located, to exist | used with inanimate objects |
| | to have | the possessed object (in English) becomes the subject with the postposition **ga** |
| | to have the characteristic of | used with the postposition **de** |
| **desu** です or **da** だ (abrupt) | to have the characteristic of, to exist | no postposition used |

### *iru* to be

The primary meaning of the verb **iru** (to be) is "to be located." It is used with living things, whether animals or humans, and if the place is specified, "in" is expressed by the postposition **ni**. The most important forms are:

**iru** いる (present)         **inai** いない (negative present)
**ita** いた (past)           **inakatta** いなかった (negative past)
**iru darō** いるだろう (probable)

Its polite forms are entirely regular:

**imasu** います (present)       **imashō** いましょう
                                or
                                **iru deshō** いるでしょう (probable)
**imashita** いました (past)     **imasen** いません (present negative)

etc. These forms are among the most common Japanese words, and you should know them.

> **Kyōshitsu ni seito ga sanjūnin imasu.**
> 教室に生徒が三十人います。
> [classroom in pupils *subj* thirty-men are]
> There are thirty pupils in the classroom.

**Otō-san wa ima uchi ni imasen.**
お父さんはいまうちにいません。
[*hon*-father as-for now house in is-not]
My father is not at home now.

**iru** used as an independent verb can only indicate location; it can not indicate quality, or number, or possession, or equality, or anything else.
**iru** is also used as an auxiliary verb to form the progressive tenses (see pages 47–48). In such cases it is translated exactly like an English progressive.

**Densha ga hashitte iru.**　　**Kare wa nani o shite imasu ka?**
電車が走っている。　　　　　　彼は何をしていますか。
[train *subj* running is]　　　[he as-for what *obj* doing is *ques*]
The train is running.　　　　　What is he doing?

*aru* **to be**
If you want to indicate the location of inanimate things, you do not use the verb **iru**. Instead, you use the verb **aru** and its forms:

**aru** ある　　　　　　　　　　　　　　(present)
**atta** あった　　　　　　　　　　　　　(past)
**arō** あろう or **aru darō** あるだろう　(probable)
**nai** ない　　　　　　　　　　　　　　(negative present, excep-
　　　　　　　　　　　　　　　　　　　　tional in form)

**nakatta** なかった　　　　　　　　　　　(negative past)
**nakarō** なかろう OR **nai darō** ないだろう　(negative probable)
**arimasu** あります　　　　　　　　　　　(present polite)
**arimashita** ありました　　　　　　　　(past polite)

etc. These forms are extremely important and you should know them.

**Shinshitsu ni wa mado ga mittsu aru.**
寝室には窓が三つある。
[bedroom in as-for windows *subj* three are]
There are three windows in the bedroom.

**Anata no gakkō wa doko ni arimasu ka ? Tōkyō ni arimasu.**
あなたの学校はどこにありますか。東京にあります。
[you of school as-for where in is *ques*] [Tōkyō in is]
Where is your school? It is in Tōkyō.

**aru** is also used to translate ideas that we express in English by "to have." In this construction, the possessed thing is made the subject of the clause and takes the postposition **ga** (see page 96 for more details).

**Okane ga arimasu ka? Arimasen.**
お金がありますか。ありません。
[hon-money *subj* is *ques*] [is-not]
Do you have any money? No, I do not have any.

*desu*

When you wish to indicate condition, or quality, or number, or characteristics, or identity, you will use the word **desu** and its more polite substitutes. **desu** is not really a verb; it is a combination of a particle and verb forms, but for our purposes it is best treated as if it were a verb. It has the following parts:

|  | ABRUPT |  | POLITE |  |
|---|---|---|---|---|
| Present | **da** | だ | **desu** | です |
| Past | **datta** | だった | **deshita** | でした |
| Probable | **darō** | だろう | **deshō** | でしょう |

When you use **desu**, you do not use the particles **wa** or **ga**, as you might expect. **desu** already has a particle within it, and needs no other:

**Kore wa boku no kippu desu.**
これは僕の切符です。
[this as-for I of ticket is]
This is my ticket.

**Watashitachi wa sannin desu.**
私達は三人です。
[we as-for, three men are]
We are three. There are three of us.

After adjectives you may use **desu** (and its forms) alone, or you may use the particle **no** (often simply **n**) after the adjective. The **no** or **n** serves to make the previous material of the sentence into a noun clause (see pages 88 ff.).

**Kare no byōki wa omoi no desu.**
彼の病気は重いのです。
[he of sickness as-for heavy one is]
His sickness is serious. He is seriously ill.

Pseudo adjectives, which are best considered nouns of a sort (see page 73), use **desu** as do other nouns. No particle is needed.

**Kirei desu ne.**
きれいですね。
[pretty is isn't-it]
It's pretty, isn't it.

**desu** has no true negative forms, and borrows forms from **aru**: **nai** (present), **nakatta** (past), **nakarō** or **nai darō** (probable). They are usually used with the postpositions **de wa**, colloquially spoken as **ja**.

**Sono firimu wa boku no de wa nai.**
そのフィルムは僕のではない。
[that film as-for I of — — is-not]
That is not my film. That film is not mine.

**desu** does not make polite forms with -**masu**. Instead, other verbs must be substituted, as you will see in the next section.

## Polite Equivalents of *desu*

**desu** and its forms are indispensable in ordinary speech, but there are occasions when more courteous equivalents are needed.* There are several such polite verbs that you can use, the most useful of which are the -**masu** forms of **aru** and **gozaru**.

---

\* This applies only to **desu** as an independent verb. When the forms **deshita** and **deshō** are used, as below, to form negative tenses, they are acceptable under almost all circumstances of courtesy. These two forms in this negative use cannot have their place taken by forms of **aru** or **gozaru**.

The polite range of forms is:

|  | POSITIVE* | NEGATIVE |
|---|---|---|
| Present | **de arimasu**<br>であります | **de wa arimasen**<br>ではありません |
| Past | **de arimashita**<br>でありました | **de wa arimasen deshita**<br>ではありませんでした |
| Probable | **de arimashō**<br><br>でありましょう | **de wa arimasen deshō**<br>(or **de wa nai deshō**)<br>ではありませんでしょう<br>(ではないでしょう) |

More courteous still are the polite forms made with **gozaru**:

|  | POSITIVE | NEGATIVE |
|---|---|---|
| Present | **gozaimasu**<br>ございます | **gozaimasen**<br>ございません |
| Past | **gozaimashita**<br>ございました | **gozaimasen deshita**<br>ございませんでした |
| Probable | **gozaimashō**<br>ございましょう | **gozaimasen deshō**<br>ございませんでしょう |

Nouns and words equivalent to nouns, like pseudo adjectives, usually take the postposition **de** to indicate the positive predicate and **de wa** to indicate the negative predicate:

| **Ikaga de gozaimasu ka?** | **Amari genki de wa gozaimasen.** |
|---|---|
| いかがでございますか。 | あまり元気ではございません。 |
| [how — are *ques*] | [too good-spirits — — are-not] |
| How are you? | Not too well, thank you. |

Adjectives, however, take special forms before the verb **gozaru**:†

**Yoroshū gozaimasu.** (from **yoroshii**)
よろしゅうございます。
[fine is]
You are right. That is right.

---

* These forms are a little too stiff for normal usage, although guides and attendants may use them to you. We include them only for recognition. Use either **desu** or **gozaimasu** forms.
† See page 63 also.

**Ohayō gozaimasu.**\* (from **hayai**)
おはようございます。
[*hon*-early are]
Good morning. (This is often abbreviated to simply **ohayō**.)

**Arigatō gozaimasu.**† (often abbreviated to simply **arigatō**)
ありがとうございます。
[difficult-to-have is]
Thank you.

## Passive and Causative Verbs

Japanese has an unusual set of verb forms that you should be able to recognize, even though it is not necessary for you to use them. These are the passive and causative forms, which are made in regular fashion from ordinary, simple verbs.

Japanese has a true passive voice (just as does Latin), which is made by adding -**reru** to the negative stem† of consonant stem (**u**-dropping) verbs, and -**rareru** to the negative stem of vowel- stem (**ru**-dropping) verbs.

|  | PRESENT FORM | NEGATIVE STEM | PASSIVE FORM |
|---|---|---|---|
| consonant stem | **kiru** 切る to cut | **kira-** | **kirareru** 切られる to be cut |
| vowel stem | **taberu** 食べる to eat | **tabe-** | **taberareru** 食べられる to be eaten |

The entire range of verb forms is then made from these forms, just as with any other vowel-conjugation (**ru**-dropping) verb. You will almost always be able to recognize a passive form by the -**are**- portion, but with the exception of the verb **umareru** (to be born) you need not bother with learning them.

The causative forms convey the idea of "caused someone to. . . ." They are formed by adding -**seru** to the negative stem of consonant-

---

\*   In these two idioms, gozaimasu is the normal courteous form you should use.

†   See page 53 ff. for a discussion of negative stems.

stem verbs, and -**saseru** to the negative stem of vowel-stem verbs. The resulting formations are conjugated like ordinary vowel-stem verbs:

**kiraseru**
切られます
to make (someone) cut

**tabesaseru**
食べさせる
to make (someone) eat

These forms, too, are given simply for recognition.

# Adjectives

## The Nature of the Japanese Adjective

The Japanese adjective is the part of speech that differs most widely from its English counterpart. It has tenses and moods, just like a verb, and is often considered to be a special type of verb. In some areas, indeed, verb forms and adjective forms overlap. All of the negative verb forms, for example, are really adjectives in origin (see page 53), as is the construction that indicates wishing or wanting to (see page 90).

Japanese adjectives can be divided into two major groups: (1) true adjectives of native Japanese origin, which are like verbs in their forms; (2) pseudo adjectives (also called quasi adjectives, adjectival nouns, and Chinese adjectives), usually of Chinese origin, which are formed quite differently, and are more closely related to nouns.

We shall discuss true adjectives first, and pseudo adjectives later (see page 73). Whenever we use the word "adjective" alone, without any qualifying term, it shall be understood that we are referring to the true, native Japanese adjectives; when we have occasion to refer to the second group of words, we shall speak of them as "pseudo adjectives."

## Adjective Forms
### Basic Stems

All Japanese adjectives, in their dictionary form, end in one of the following four sounds: -**ai**, -**ii**, -**oi**, -**ui**. They form their basic stem by dropping the -**i**:

| ADJECTIVE | | MEANING | BASIC STEM |
|---|---|---|---|
| **akai** | 赤い | red | **aka-** |
| **atsui** | 暑い | hot | **atsu-** |
| **samui** | 寒い | cold | **samu-** |
| **kuroi** | 黒い | black | **kuro-** |
| **shiroi** | 白い | white | **shiro-** |
| **utsukushii** | 美しい | pretty | **utsukushi-** |

This basic stem is used to make all the other forms of the adjective.

We shall not describe all the forms that can be made for each adjective; instead, as we do with verbs, we shall describe only those important forms that you are likely to hear. These forms are the present, the past, the probable, the adverbial, the suspending, the conditional, and the negative.

## Present Forms

The present form of an adjective is the form that you will find given in dictionaries:

| | | | | | | |
|---|---|---|---|---|---|---|
| **ii** (or **yoi**) | 良い | good | **warui** | 悪い | bad |
| **hayai** | 早い | fast | **osoi** | 遅い | slow |
| **furui** | 古い | old | **wakai** | 若い | young |
| **atarashii** | 新しい | new | **nagai** | 長い | long |

This is the form that is used to modify a noun:

| | | |
|---|---|---|
| **atarashii kutsu** | 新しい靴 | new shoes |
| **ii tenki** | いい天気 | good weather |
| **shiroi hana** | 白い花 | white flowers |

Since adjectives are closely related to verbs in Japanese, each adjective is considered to have a part of the verb "to be" within it, and can be used without any true verb:

**Sono kutsu wa atarashii.**
その靴は新しい。
[those shoes as-for new]
Those shoes are new.

**Kono niwa wa utsukushii.**
この庭は美しい。
[this garden as-for beautiful]
This garden is beautiful.

## Past Forms

Adjectives form a past tense by adding -**katta** to their basic stem:

| PRESENT ADJECTIVE | PAST ADJECTIVE |
|---|---|
| **takai** 高い high (price or height) | **takakatta** 高かった was high |
| **yasui** 安い cheap | **yasukatta** 安かった was cheap |

These forms can also be used without forms of a verb:

**Kyonen wa denshachin ga yasukatta.**
去年は電車賃が安かった。
[last-year as-for train-fare *subj* was-cheap(er)]
Last year's train fare was cheaper.

These adjective past forms may also be used to modify nouns:

**Kyonen takakatta denshachin wa . . .**
去年高かった電車賃は…
[last-year was-high train-fare as-for . . .]
As for last year's train fare, which was expensive, . . .

In such instances, the past tense is usually translated into English as a relative clause (see page 86 for relative clauses).

**Probable Mood**
The probable tense is formed by adding -**karō** to the basic stem.

PRESENT ADJECTIVE                    PROBABLE ADJECTIVE
**samui** 寒い cold                   **samukarō** 寒かろう is probably cold

**Fuyu wa kono heya wa samukarō.**
冬はこの部屋は寒かろう。
[winter as-for this room as-for probably-cold]
This room is probably cold in the winter.

The probable mood expresses a way of thought that is peculiar to Japanese. It is used to indicate a probability, either in the present or the future, a wonderment or doubt on the part of the speaker, and similar concepts. The sentence above could be translated equally well as: I wonder if this room is cold in the winter, I think this room is cold in the winter, etc. These feelings are closely related to those of the probable forms of the verb (see page 48), although with adjectives there obviously can be no emphatic meanings such as the verb often has.

All of these three forms of the adjective—the present, the past, and the probable—are what are called final forms. They can be used to complete a sentence or a clause.

In actual usage, however, these forms are considered somewhat abrupt if they are used at the end of a sentence, although they are perfectly acceptable as modifiers for nouns or in relative clauses. It is better to avoid them at the end of a sentence, by making use of one of the following more courteous possible substitutions.

(1) Add **desu**, "to be" (past **deshita**, probable **deshō**) to the present tense of the adjective.

(2) Add **no desu** (past **no deshita**, probable **no deshō**) to the present tense of the adjective. In colloquial speech the **no** is often abbreviated to **n**.

(3) Add **gozaimasu** (past **gozaimashita**, probable **gozaimashō**) to a special form of the adjective.

These forms are arranged in order of their courtesy:

**Kono hana shiroi.**　　　　　[abrupt]
この花白い。
[This flower as-for white]
This flower is white.

**Kono hana wa shiroi desu.**　　[normal]
この花は白いです。

**Kono hana wa shiroi no desu.**　[normal]
この花は白いのです。

**Kono hana wa shirō gozaimasu.**　[very courteous]
この花は白うございます。

All of these sentences convey the same thought and differ only in courtesy or formality. The formations are explained in more detail in the section on equivalents to the English verb "to be" (see page 57).

As you have probably noticed, the adjective before **gozaimasu** has a special ending. These special endings are used only with forms of **gozaru**. They are made from the adverbial form of the adjective (see page 69), but their formation is somewhat complex. It is easier to use the following table:

| EXAMPLES | ADJECTIVES ENDING IN | CHANGE THE ENDING TO | AND FORM |
|---|---|---|---|
| **osoi**<br>遅い<br>late | -oi | -ō | **osō**<br>遅う |
| **hayai**<br>早い<br>fast | -ai | -ō | **hayō**<br>早う |
| **atarashii**<br>新しい<br>new | -ii | -ū | **atarashū**<br>新しゅう |
| **samui**<br>寒い<br>cold | -ui | -ū | **samū**<br>寒う |

**Sono jidōsha wa atarashū gozaimasu ka?**
その自動車は新しゅうございますか。
[that auto as-for new is *ques*]
Is that auto new?

**Ohayō gozaimasu.**
おはようございます
[*hon*-early are]
Good morning.

**Kinō wa samū gozaimashita.**
きのうは寒うございました。
[yesterday as-for cold was]
Yesterday it was cold.

Note that this form is used when only extreme courtesy is intended. **Ohayō gozaimasu,** however, is an idiom, and is normal usage. You would not say **ohayai desu**.

## Adverbial Forms

Adverbs are normally made from adjectives by adding the suffix -**ku** to the stem, or, to phrase it differently, by changing the final -**i** of the adjective to -**ku**:

| PRESENT ADJECTIVE | STEM | ADVERBIAL FORM |
|---|---|---|
| **omoshiroi**<br>面白い<br>interesting | omoshiro- | **omoshiroku**<br>面白く<br>interestingly |
| **osoi**<br>遅い<br>late | oso- | **osoku**<br>遅く<br>late [adverb] |

| PRESENT ADJECTIVE | STEM | ADVERBIAL FORM |
|---|---|---|
| **ii** (or **yoi**) | **yo-** | **yoku** |
| 良い | 良く | |
| good | well | |
| | | |
| **hayai** | **haya-** | **hayaku** |
| 早い | 早く | |
| quick, rapid | quickly, rapidly | |

| | |
|---|---|
| **Omoshiroku kikoemasu.** | **Yoku dekita.** |
| 面白く聞こえます | 良く出来た。 |
| [interestingly sounds] | [well existed] |
| It sounds interesting. | Well done! |

Japanese is stricter about associating the adverbial form with a verb than is English, as can be seen from the first sentence: **omoshiroku kikoemasu**. We, in English, feel that the state described in this sentence is really a matter of "being," hence not an adverb; Japanese feels that since the word is associated with a verb, the word should be an adverb.

The adverbial form of the adjective, as we shall see later, is also the base from which the negative adjectival forms are made, and, with some contraction and assimilation, the base for tenses, moods, and incomplete forms.

### Suspending Form

The suspending form of the adjective is the form that corresponds (in some respects) to the participle of a verb. It is either the same as the adverbial form or is the adverbial form plus -**te**:

| PRESENT ADJECTIVE | ADVERBIAL FORM | SUSPENDING FORM |
|---|---|---|
| **aoi** 青い blue, green | **aoku** 青く | **aokute** 青くて |

**Sono ringo wa aokute, katai deshō.**
そのリンゴは青くて、硬いでしょう。
[those apples as-for green-being, hard probably-are]
Those apples are green and are probably hard.

These suspending forms cannot be used at the end of a sentence (which calls for a final form). They are only used in incomplete clauses (without conjunctions) within sentences. For more detail on their use, see page 83 where continuative forms of adjectives and verbs are discussed.

You could also use the present tense of the adjective followed by the words **no de** (in this case, an equivalent to a participle of the verb "to be") instead of the suspending form:

**Sono ringo ga aoi no de, katai deshō.**
そのリンゴが青いので、硬いでしょう。
[those apples sj green being, hard probably-are]
Because these apples are non-ripe ("green"), they are probably hard.

**Adjectives and Conditions**
The easiest way of expressing a conditional form of an adjective is by using the word **nara** (or **naraba**) (meaning "if") with the present or past of the adjective:

| | | |
|---|---|---|
| **samui nara** | 寒いなら | if it is cold |
| **atsui nara** | 暑いなら | if it is hot |
| **samukatta nara** | 寒かったなら | if it was cold |

There are also true conditional forms, however, which you should be able to recognize. They are made in much the same way as true verb conditionals: (1) for a present conditional, add -**kereba** to the basic stem; (2) for a past conditional, add -**ra** to the final past.

| | | |
|---|---|---|
| **samukereba** | 寒ければ | if it is cold |
| **samukattara** | 寒かったら | if it was cold |

**Samukereba uwagi o ki nasai.**
寒ければ上着を着なさい。
[if-it-is-cold jacket *obj* wear please]
If it is cold, put on your jacket.

**Atsui nara mado o akemashō ka?**
暑いなら窓を開けましょうか。
[hot if window *obj* probably-open *ques*]
If it is hot, shall I open the window?

**Negative Adjectives**

Negative adjectives are made in the same way as negative verbs: by adding the proper form of the word **nai** to a stem, in this case the adverbial stem:

| | | |
|---|---|---|
| Pres. adj. | **omoshiroi**<br>面白い | amusing, interesting,<br>  noteworthy |
| Adv. form | **omoshiroku**<br>面白く | amusingly, interestingly,<br>  being noteworthy |
| Pres. final<br>neg. | **omoshiroku nai**<br>面白くない | is not interesting |
| Past final<br>neg. | **omoshiroku nakatta**<br>面白くなかった | was not interesting |
| Cond. neg. | **omoshiroku nakereba**<br>面白くなければ | if it is not interesting |
| | **omoshiroku nakattara**<br>面白くなかったら | if it was not interesting |
| Susp. neg. | (**omoshiroku nakute**)<br>(面白くなくて) | not being interesting |
| | (**omoshiroku naku**)<br>(面白くなく) | not being interesting |
| Prob. neg. | **omoshiroku nakarō**<br>面白くなかろう | it probably is not interesting |

All of these conjugational forms, however, are abrupt, and more courteous forms are often substituted for them. These courteous forms are those of the negative conjugation of the verb, and range through **desu** and **de aru** to **gozaru**.

| | PRESENT | PAST |
|---|---|---|
| Conjugational<br>form: | **omoshiroku nai**<br>面白くない | **omoshiroku nakatta**<br>面白くなかった |
| (More courteous) | **omoshiroku nai desu**<br>面白くないです | **omoshiroku nakatta desu**<br>面白くなかったです |
| (More courteous) | **omoshiroku arimasen**<br>面白くありません | **omoshiroku arimasen<br>  deshita**<br>面白くありませんでした |

|          | PRESENT | PAST |
|----------|---------|------|
| (Polite) | **omoshirō gozaimasen**<br>面白うございません | **omoshirō gozaimasen deshita**<br>面白うございませんでした |

The following table recapitulates the more important forms of a Japanese adjective:

| PRESENT ADJECTIVE | BASIC STEM |
|-------------------|------------|
| **oishii** (tasty, delicious) | **oishi-** |

|               | POSITIVE | NEGATIVE |
|---------------|----------|----------|
| Present final | **oishii**<br>おいしい | **oishiku nai**<br>おいしくない |
| Adverbial | **oishiku**<br>おいしく | **oishiku naku**<br>おいしくなく |
| Past final | **oishikatta**<br>おいしかった | **oishiku nakatta**<br>おいしくなかった |
| Conditional | **oishikereba**<br>おいしければ | **oishiku nakereba**<br>おいしくなければ |
|  | **oishikattara**<br>おいしかったら | **oishiku nakattara**<br>おいしくなかったら |
| Suspending | **oishiku**<br>おいしく | **oishiku naku**<br>おいしくなく |
|  | **oishikute**<br>おいしくて | **oishiku nakute**<br>おいしくなくて |
| Probable | **oishikarō**<br>おししかろう | **oishiku nakarō**<br>おいしくなかろう |
| Polite form for combination with **gozaru** | **oishū (gozaimasu)**<br>おいしゅう（ございます） | **oishū (gozaimasen)**<br>おいしゅう（ございません） |

## Pseudo Adjectives

In addition to the true Japanese adjectives, which are like verbs in many ways, there are other Japanese forms that convey adjectival meanings (and which we translate as adjectives) even though the English classification does not really apply to them. These forms fall

into two groups: (1) nouns and pronouns used in adjectival constructions; (2) pseudo adjectives or noun-like words that are used with
special postpositions to convey an adjectival meaning.

Japanese is by no means as rich in adjectives as English, and many
ideas that we can express with an adjective must be expressed in
Japanese by noun phrases with the postposition **no** corresponding to
the English construction "of. . ."

**Amerika no shufu**
アメリカの首府
[United States of capital]
the American capital

**Nihon no ocha**
日本のお茶
[Japan of tea]
Japanese tea

**tetsu no fune**
鉄の船
[iron of ship]
an iron ship, a ship of iron

**kinu no kimono**
絹の着物
[silk of clothing]
silken clothing, clothing of silk

Adjectives for the pronouns are formed in this way, too:

**boku no inu**
僕の犬
[I of dog]
my dog

**anata no namae**
あなたの名前
[you of name]
your name

**donata no tegami**
どなたの手紙
[who of letter]
whose letter

This same construction includes some ideas that we consider adverbial in English:

**koko no hon**
ここの本
[here of book]
this book (here)

The pseudo adjectives, most of which are Chinese in origin, are
very numerous and are used in most situations where abstract ideas
are concerned, just as in English we use French or Latin forms for

learned words. These pseudo adjectives have their own peculiar particles, which in many cases reflect older forms that have disappeared elsewhere. They are basically nouns, however, and in normal sentences require verbs to complete their meaning.

A few of the more common pseudo adjectives are:

| | | | | | |
|---|---|---|---|---|---|
| **kirei** | きれい | beautiful | **rippa** | 立派 | splendid |
| **rikō** | りこう | intelligent | **shizuka** | 静か | quiet |
| **chōhō** | 重宝 | useful | **kekkō** | 結構 | splendid, nice, fine |

When these pseudo adjectives are used to modify nouns, the particle **na** is added to them:

**kirei na onna**
きれいな女
beautiful — woman

**rikō na ko**
りこうな子
intelligent — child

When they are used adverbially, they take the particle **ni**:

**Kare wa kirei ni ji o kakimasu.**
彼はきれいに字を書きます。
[he as-for beautiful — characters *obj* writes]
He writes letters [Japanese characters] beautifully.

**kyū ni**
急に
suddenly

**Kanojo wa kyū ni warai-dashimashita.**
彼女は急に笑い出した。
[she as-for suddenly — laugh-began]
She suddenly began to laugh.

**genki ni**
元気に
vigorously

**Motto genki ni aruki nasai.**
もっと元気に歩きなさい。
[more vigorously — walk please]
Please walk more rapidly.

Just as the adverbial forms ending in -**ku** (in true adjectives) are used before verbs meaning "to become" or "to seem" or "to appear," the pseudo-adjectival forms with **ni** are used in the same situations:

**rikō ni mieru**
りこうに見える
[intelligent — look]
to look intelligent

In most other situations these pseudo adjectives are treated like nouns.

(1) Where a true adjective would require a suspending form (at the end of an incomplete clause, perhaps), pseudo adjectives need a suspending form of one of the verbs meaning "to be." **de** is the form normally used:

| | |
|---|---|
| **shizuka de** | **Kono heya wa shizuka de ii.** |
| 静かで | この部屋は静かでいい。 |
| [quiet being] | [this room as-for quiet being good] |
| Since this room is quiet, it is good. | This room being quiet, it is good. |

(2) The final forms (corresponding to the final forms of a true adjective) are made by adding one of the final forms of a verb meaning "to be":

**Kirei da.**          (abrupt)
きれいだ。
[beautiful is]
It's beautiful.

**Kirei desu.**          (normal)
きれいです。

**Kirei de gozaimasu.**    (very polite)
きれいでございます。

The past, probable, and negative forms can be expressed by changing the verb part.

| | |
|---|---|
| **Kirei deshita.** | **Kirei de wa nai.** |
| きれいでした。 | きれいではない。 |
| [beautiful was] | [beautiful being as-for not-is] |
| It was beautiful. | It is not beautiful. |

Note that you do not add **no** before **desu,** as you might with a true adjective; nor do you make sound changes before **gozaimasu.** **Kirei** is a noun, actually; it never changes, and does not need a nominalizing particle.

(3) The conditional is made with **nara** or **naraba.**

**Kirei nara . . .**
きれいなら…
[beautiful if]
If it is beautiful . . .

Two true adjectives, **okii** (large, big) and **chiisai** (small), are also occasionally pseudo adjectives. When modifying nouns, they can take the ending **na,** although the ordinary ending -**i** is equally common:

| | | | |
|---|---|---|---|
| **okii me** | 大きい目 | **chiisai kuchi** | 小さい口 |
| **okina me** | 大きな目 | **chiisana kuchi** | 小さな口 |
| large eyes | | small mouth | |

## Comparison of Adjectives

Comparisons are expressed in a highly idiomatic way in Japanese. Indeed, it is sometimes difficult for an English speaker to recognize that a comparison has been made, unless he has memorized the proper speech pattern.

Strictly speaking, Japanese adjectives and pseudo adjectives do not have special forms for comparative and superlative ideas. In some cases the words **motto** (more) and **mottomo** (most) or **ichiban** (number one) can be used before an adjective or pseudo adjective, to convey the idea of comparison, but the result may not always be idiomatic. It is better if you memorize a few special patterns that you are likely to meet.

If you wish to say, "A is cheaper than B," you must phrase your sentence in this fashion: "A **wa** B **yori** cheap is."

**Ringo wa ume yori yasui desu.**
リンゴはウメより安いです。
[apples as-for, plums than, cheap is]
Apples are cheaper than plums.

"Which is cheaper, A or B?" you must phrase as "A **to** B **to wa dochira ga** cheap."

**Ringo to momo to wa dochira ga yasui desu ka?**
リンゴとモモとはどちらが安いですか。
[apples with peaches with as-for which *subj* cheap is *ques*]
Which are cheaper, apples or peaches?

"A is cheaper" you should phrase as "A is cheap."

| | |
|---|---|
| **Ringo wa yasui desu.**    or | **Ringo wa motto yasui desu.** |
| リンゴは安いです。 | リンゴはもっと安いです。 |
| [apples as-for cheap are] | [apples as-for more cheap are] |
| Apples are cheaper. | Apples are cheaper. |

Superlatives are made in the same fashion; **mottomo** or **ichiban** may be added for clarity:

| | |
|---|---|
| **Ringo wa mottomo yasui desu.**  or | **Ringo wa ichiban yasui desu.** |
| リンゴはもっとも安いです。 | リンゴはいちばん安いです。 |
| [apples as-for most cheap are] | [apples as-for number-1 cheap are] |
| Apples are the cheapest. | Apples are the cheapest. |

Sometimes the phrase **no hō** (—'s direction) is added to the main article being compared:

**Ringo no hō ga, momo yori, yasui desu.**
リンゴの方が、モモより、安いです。
[apples of direction *subj* peaches than cheap is]
Apples are cheaper than peaches.

**Ringo to ume to wa, dochira no hō ga yasui desu ka?**
リンゴとウメとは、どちらの方が安いですか。
[apples with plums with as-for which of direction *subj* cheap is *ques*]
Which are cheaper, apples or plums?

**Ringo no hō ga yasui desu.**
リンゴの方が安いです。
[apples of direction cheap is]
Apples are cheaper.

"As . . . as . . ." is equally idiomatic; it is expressed by setting one of the two objects apart with the particle **wa,** placing **to onaji hodo** after the second, and then expressing a normal sentence with the remaining ideas.

**Nashi wa ringo to onaji hodo yasui desu.**
ナシはリンゴと同じほど安いです。
[pears as-for apples with same degree cheap is]
Pears are as cheap as apples.

# Adverbs

The words which we normally translate into English as adverbs are very often other parts of speech in Japanese, where there are few true adverbs. We have already stated (see page 69) that each adjective has an adverbial form. There are also some nouns that form phrases that are best translated as adverbs.

Many words of time and place are intermediate between nouns and adverbs in their usage:

| | | | | | |
|---|---|---|---|---|---|
| **kyō** | 今日 | today | **ashita** | あした | (or **asu** あす) tomorrow |
| **kinō** | きのう | yesterday | **koko** | ここ | here |
| **soko** | そこ | there | **asoko** | あそこ | there in the distance |

These words may be used with the particle **wa**, or they may be used with **no** to indicate attribution:

**ashita no ryokō**
あしたの旅行
[tomorrow of trip]
the trip tomorrow

**koko no tegami**
ここの手紙
[here of letter]
the letter here

The participles of some verbs have also become frozen into adverbial meanings:

| | | |
|---|---|---|
| **kaette** | かえって | on the contrary, rather, all the more |
| **aikawarazu** | 相変わらず | as usual, as before |
| **kesshite** | けっして | never |
| **mattaku** | まったく | not at all |

**Undō ga kaette gai ni natta.**
運動がかえって害になった。
[exercise *subj* on-the-contrary harm to became]
The exercise did more harm than good.

**Watashi wa aikawarazu isogashii.**
私は相変わらず忙しい。
[I as-for as-usual busy]
I am busy as usual.

**Kesshite sonna koto wa shimasen.**
けっしてそんな事はしません。
[never such things as-for do-not]
I never do such things. I shall never do such things.

**Mattaku shirimasen.**
まったく知りません。
[at-all know-not]
I do not know at all. I have no idea.

The following true adverbs are also important:

| | | | | | | |
|---|---|---|---|---|---|---|
| **taihen** | 大変 | very | **shika**\* | しか | only | |
| (or **taisō**) | (たいそう) | | | | | |
| **mada** | まだ | yet | **naze** | なぜ | why | |
| **yagate** | やがて | soon | **mō** | もう | already | |
| **ikaga** | いかが | how | **yukkuri** | ゆっくり | slowly | |
| **sukoshi** | 少し | a little | **bakkari** | ばっかり | only | |
| **motto** | もっと | more | **takusan** | たくさん | much, many, a lot | |

Other adverbs are formed from the demonstrative pronouns (see pages 30 ff.):

| | | | | | |
|---|---|---|---|---|---|
| **dō** | どう | how? | **doko** | どこ | where |
| **kō** | こう | like this | **doko ka** | どこか | somewhere |
| **sō** | そう | so, thus | **doko mo**\* | どこも | nowhere |

These forms are covered in more detail in the section on demonstrating words (see pages 30 ff.).

**taihen atsui**            **Kare wa mada kite imasen.**
大変暑い                   彼はまだ来ていません。
very hot                    [he as-for not-yet coming is-not]
                           He has not come yet.

---

\* With a negative verb.

**Yagate haru desu.**
やがて春です。
[soon spring is]
It will soon be spring.

**Sukoshi kudasai.**
少しください。
[little please-give]
Give me a little, please.

**Kore shika motte imasen.**
これしか持っていません。
[this only having is-not]
I have only this.

**Mō natsu desu.**
もう夏です。
[already summer is]
It is already summer.

**Sukoshi dake kudasai.**
少しだけください。
[little only please-give]
Please give me just a little.

**Dō shimashō ka?**
どうしましょうか。
[how shall-do *ques*]
How shall I do it?

**Doko ni arimasu ka?**
どこにありますか。
[where in is *ques*]
Where is it?

**Ikaga desu ka?**
いかがですか。
[how is *ques*]
How are you?

**Motto kudasai.**
もっとください。
[more please-give]
Please give me some more.

**Naze desu ka?**
なぜですか。
[why is *ques*]
Why is it so?

**Yukkuri hanashite kudasai.**
ゆっくり話してください。
[slowly speaking please]
Please speak slowly.

**Takusan kudasai.**
たくさんください。
[much please-give]
Please give me a lot.

**Sō omoimasu. Sō desu ka?**
そう思います。そうですか。
[so think] [so is *ques*]
I think so. Is that so?

**Doko-ni-mo ikimasen.**
どこにも行きません。
[in-no-where go-not]
I am not going anywhere.

# Verb Constructions and Adjective Constructions

**Final and Medial Forms of Verbs and Adjectives**

Every complete sentence in Japanese must end with a final verb or adjective form. These final forms are:

present (positive and negative)
present progressive (positive and negative) for verbs
past (positive and negative)
past progressive (positive and negative) for verbs
probable (positive and negative)
probable progressive (positive and negative) for verbs
imperatives

Of these forms above, both the polite forms ending in -**masu** and its developments and the abrupt conjugational forms are considered final.

The following forms are medial, and cannot end a complete sentence:

the participle
the conditional (either the true conditional formed from a verb, or the substitutes with **nara** or **to**)
verb stems when used independently

In adjectives, the adverb forms, the continuative forms, the conditionals, and the coalesced forms used with **gozaru** are medial, and cannot end a complete sentence.

This may seem complex at first, but actually English has much the same situation. An English independent clause cannot stand with a participle alone, nor can a conditional sense or other concessive sense.

**Kare wa hon o yonde imasu.**
彼は本を読んでいます。
[he as-for book *obj* reading is]
He is reading a book.

**yonde imasu** is a present progressive tense, and is able to end a sentence.

**Sora wa aoku, kumo wa shiroi.**
空は青く、雲は白い。
[sky as-for blue, clouds as-for white]
The sky is blue, the clouds are white.

**aoku** is an adverbial form and could not occur at the end of the sentence; **shiroi** is a present form and could not occur independently within the sentence.

## Clauses and Verb Forms

In English we can form sentences out of various combinations of dependent and independent clauses. We can have a dependent clause ("When I opened the door . . .") together with an independent clause ("it was raining outside"). Or we can use two independent clauses: ("I opened the door and it was raining outside."). Japanese, however, can not combine independent clauses in this way; all sentences that are not simple sentences must be built up out of dependent clauses and only one independent clause. The independent clause must come at the end of the sentence.

**Mado o aketa toki ame ga futte imashita.**
窓を開けたとき雨が降っていました。
[window *obj* opened when rain *subj* falling was]
When I opened the window, it was raining. I opened the window and
  it was raining.

Dependent clauses are formed in one of two ways: (1) their verb is a participle, or, in the case of adjectives, the continuative form.

**Uchi e kite shokuji o shimasen ka?** (participle, **kite**)
うちへ来て食事をしませんか。
[house to coming meal *obj* do-not *ques*]
Won't you come to my house and have dinner?

**Bara wa akaku, yuri wa shiroi.** (continuative form, **akaku**, from **akai**)
バラは赤く、ユリは白い。
[roses as-for red, lilies as-for white]
Roses are red, but lilies are white.

Several of these participle forms may occur in a series.

**Ryōriya ni haitte, kondate o mite, oyako-donburi o chūmon shi-mashita.**
料理屋に入って、献立を見て、親子丼ぶりを注文しました。
[restaurant in entering, menu *obj* looking-at, oyako-domburi *obj* order did]
I went into a restaurant, looked at the menu, and finally ordered oyako-donburi (a rice dish containing chicken and eggs).

Translation of these forms depends upon the context of the sentence:

**Sono eiga wa mijikakute omoshiroi.**
その映画は短くて面白い。
[that movie as-for short interesting]
That movie is short but interesting. Although the movie is short, it is interesting.

(2) The second way of forming dependent clauses is to use certain conjunctions, most of which take final forms. We shall discuss these conjunctions in more detail elsewhere, and shall merely list them here:

| | | |
|---|---|---|
| **ga** | が | but, and |
| **to*** | と | when, if; that |
| **keredomo** | けれども | but |
| **aida** | あいだ | at the same time, while |
| **kara** | から | because |
| **no de** | ので | since, because |
| **ato-†** | 後 | after |
| **mae*†** | 前 | before |
| **no ni** | のに | even though |
| **tokoro de** | ところで | at the same time as |

---

\* Can be used only with present forms of verbs
† Can be used only with verbs.

| | | |
|---|---|---|
| **nara** | なら | if |
| **toki** | とき | when, whenever |

Two conjunctions, however, take the participle to form dependent clauses:

**kara**   after (only in this meaning)
**mo**   even if; neither . . . nor (with negative verb)

**Shokuji o shite kara dekakemasu.**
食事をしてから出かけます。
[dinner *obj* doing after leave]
After I have had dinner, I shall leave.

**Ame ga futte mo watashi wa dekakemasu.**
雨が降っても私は出かけます。
[rain *subj* falling even, I as-for go-out]
Even if it is raining, I will go out.

There is a third way of forming dependent clauses, using such conjugational forms as the true conditional and similar forms, but for the purposes of this simple discussion, these forms shall be ignored. It is enough if you recognize a true conditional form if you hear it.

### Final Forms and Relative Clauses
The Japanese relative clause is a very idiomatic construction. There are no relative pronouns in Japanese, and such words as *who, that, in which, where,* and *when,* when used in a relative sense, are not translated. Instead, the relative clause is treated as if it were one elaborate adjective, and is placed in front of the word which it modifies. This may seem strange at first, but actually it is not at all illogical: in function a relative clause is very much like an adjective.

Before giving Japanese examples, we shall give a few English paraphrases, so that you will see how the ideas occur:

ENGLISH
the porter who carried our luggage
the place where we bought the stamps
an automobile that is old

an island with trees that are high
the book that he wrote

JAPANESE
[the] our-luggage-carried porter
[the] we-the-stamps-bought place
[an] old-automobile
[a] trees-high island
[the] he-wrote book

In relative clauses, polite verb and adjective forms are usually not used. Instead, you usually use the normal conjugational forms of the verb or adjective. This is not felt to be discourteous, since the politeness or courtesy in the final verb of the sentence covers the previous verbs.

**Kare no\* kaita hon . . .**
彼の書いた本…
[he *subj* wrote book]
The book that he wrote . . .

**Takai ki no\* aru shima . . .**
高い木のある島…
[high trees *subj* are island]
An island on which there are high trees . . . An island with trees that are high . . . etc.

**Kesa anata no mita Asahi (Shinbun). . .**
けさあなたの見た朝日（新聞）…
[this-morning you *subj* saw Asahi]
The Asahi [newspaper] that you saw this morning . . .

Relative clauses have two peculiarities. (1) The postposition **ga** is not used to indicate the subject. Instead, **no** is used. This is really less significant than it seems, since **ga** and **no** are historically the same particle. (2) The verbs in relative clauses, according to context, can be used to convey active or passive ideas when translated into English.

---

\*    **no** is often used instead of **ga** in relative clauses. See below.

**Boku no kaita tegami . . .**
僕の書いた手紙…
[I *subj* written letter]
The letter that was written by me . . .
The letter that I wrote . . .

In English we distinguish sharply between the two ideas of activeness or passiveness. In Japanese the verb, as we have mentioned earlier, is neutral in most cases, since it partakes of the nature of a noun.

## Nominalization and Final Forms

Nominalization is one of the most difficult constructions in Japanese, since to a Western mind it often seems entirely unexpected, arbitrary, and logically inexplicable. To explain it on the simplest level, it consists of taking a phrase, a clause, or even a sentence, and turning it into a clause modifying a special word called a nominalizer. The nominalizer and the material that modifies it is then treated like a noun, and may become the subject or object of a further sentence.

Three nominalizers are in general use: **koto**, fact or situation; **mono**, thing, person; **no**, thing or one. (Do not confuse this **no** with the particle **no**.) The abrupt forms of the verb and adjective are used before them.

Let us give some examples of this in English words, before quoting Japanese examples:

Simple: I walked down the street.
Nominalized: I-walked-down-the-street-situation exists.
   (My walking down the street took place. It is a fact that I walked down the street. A situation in which I walked down the street existed.)

Simple: The apples were green.
Nominalized: The-apples-were-green-situation existed.

The use of nominalizers is very complex, and it will be sufficient if you recognize them for what they are when you hear them. You can, however, bear the following points in mind: (1) **no** can often be translated as "one": **Tōkyō kara no wa**, "the one from Tōkyō." (2) **no** or its short form **n** is the normal way of connecting an abrupt adjective form with a verb of being, to make a more courteous form:

| | |
|---|---|
| **Ame ga tsumetai.** | **Ame ga tsumetai no desu.** |
| 雨が冷たい。 | 雨が冷たいのです。 |
| [rain *subj* cold] | [rain *subj* cold one is] |
| The rain is cold. | The rain is cold. |

(3) **koto** is normally used in idioms to express ability and the idea of ever-never:

**Hashi de taberu koto ga dekimasu ka?**
箸で食べる事ができますか。
[chopsticks with eat fact *subj* is-able *ques*]
Can you eat with chopsticks ?

**Sō iu hanashi o kiita koto ga arimasen.**
そういう話を聞いたことがありません。
[such speak story *obj* heard fact *subj* is-not]
I have never heard such a story.

**Kare to hanasanakatta\* koto ga zannen desu.**
彼と話さなかったことが残念です。
[him with did-not-speak fact *subj* disappointment is]
The fact that I did not speak to him is regrettable. I am sorry that I did not speak to him.

These two constructions ("ability" and "ever") are explained in more detail on pages 95 and 96, respectively.

It may help you to remember these constructions if you recognize that these nominalizing clauses are closely related to relative clauses, which in turn are related to both adjectives and dependent clauses governed by conjunctions. The basic idea behind them all is that it is possible to isolate great blocks of thought and either set them off as entities, or subordinate them to other thoughts or words. We do this to a certain extent in English, too, though such phenomena as noun clauses are more literary than colloquial: "That the Government is a scoundrel has long been plain to us." In Japanese, on the other hand,

---

\* Past negative of **hanasu**, to speak.

such balances and equations and dissociations are the height of being colloquial.

## Special Verb Ideas and Idioms
### Wishing

Japanese does not express the concept of wishing or wanting to do something in the same way that we do. Instead, it adds a special suffix, the adjectival form -**tai**, to the combining stem of the verb you wish to use. -**tai** is treated just like any other adjective, with the full range of true (somewhat abrupt) forms and polite equivalents (see page 116).

| PRESENT | | COMBIN-ING STEM | WISH FORM |
|---|---|---|---|
| Consonant conjugation: **kaku** | to write | **kaki-** | **kakitai** 書きたい |
| Vowel conjugation: **taberu** | to eat | **tabe-** | **tabetai** 食べたい |

To list the major forms of this construction:

| | NORMAL (ABRUPT) | POLITE |
|---|---|---|
| Present | **kakitai**<br>書きたい<br>I wish to write. | **kakitai no desu** (ordinary)<br>書きたいのです |
| | | **kakitō gozaimasu** (courteous)<br>書きとうございます |
| Past | **kakitakatta**<br>書きたかった<br>I wished to write. | **kakitakatta no desu**<br>書きたかったのです |
| | | **kakitō gozaimashita**<br>書きとうございました |
| Present<br>negative | **kakitaku nai**<br>書きたくない<br>I do not wish to write. | **kakitaku arimasen**<br>書きたくありません |
| | | **kakitō gozaimasen**<br>書きとうございません |
| Past negative | **kakitaku nakatta**<br>書きたくなかった<br>I did not wish to write. | **kakitaku arimasen deshita**<br>書きたくありませんでした |
| | | **kakitō gozaimasen deshita**<br>書きとうございませんでした |

You will discover that there is a good deal of diversity in the particles that are used with these -**tai** forms. The easiest speech pattern for you to follow, however, is to set off the English subject with **wa**, turn the English object into a grammatical subject with **ga**, and think of the -**tai** form as if it were an adjective.

**Boku wa ringo ga kaitai.**
僕はリンゴが買いたい。
[I as-for apples *subj* buy-want]
I want to buy some apples.

## "If"-Statements

The easiest way to form a conditional clause in Japanese is by using the word **nara** (or **naraba**) as if it were a conjunction meaning "if." It is placed at the end of the if-clause, which is constructed normally, with the verb in a final abrupt form (past or present):

**Kare ga iku nara boku mo ikimasu.**
彼が行くなら僕も行きます。
[he *subj* go if, I also go]
If he goes, I shall go, too.

**Tsukarete iru nara, oyasumi nasai.**
疲れているなら、お休みなさい。
[tired-being are if, *hon*-rest do]
If you are tired, take a rest, please.

This construction can be used to express any of the possible "if" constructions that exist in English, including contrary-to-fact statements. Japanese does not have the sharp distinction between ordinary conditions and contrary-to-fact conditions that English has. In contrary-to-fact statements, however, you must be careful to put the verbs in the proper logical time forms, rather than follow English modes.

**nara** is really a verb form in origin, and a peculiarity of its use is that it contains within it the idea of the verb "to be." It can therefore be used directly after nouns, pronouns, pseudo adjectives, and adjectives, without other verb forms:

**Asu wa ii tenki nara . . .**
あすはいい天気なら…
[tomorrow as-for good weather if. . .]
If the weather is good tomorrow . . .

**Boku nara . . .**
僕なら
[I if . . .]
If it were I . . .

**Sake wa amari tsuyoi nara . . .**
酒はあまり強いなら…
[sake as-for too strong if . . .]
If sake is too strong for you . . .

The word **moshi** is often used to strengthen the feeling of the conditional statement; it is placed at the beginning of the clause:

**Moshi kare ga iku nara boku mo ikimasu.**
もし彼が行くなら僕も行きます。
[if he *subj* go if, I also go]
If he goes, I shall go, too.

Another easy way of forming a conditional is with the conjunction **to**, which can be translated "if," "in case," or sometimes "when" (when the idea of time is not too strong). **to** is placed at the end of the if-clause, and the present abrupt final forms of the verb (or adjective) are used.

**Kono hon o yomu to . . .**
この本を読むと…
[this book *obj* read if . . .]
If you read this book, . . .

The **nara** form is probably the easiest for you to use, but in modern colloquial Japanese the true conditional forms that verbs and adjectives make are more commonly used. You should be able to recognize them, even if you find the **nara** construction easier to use.

The true conditional forms are very regular. The present conditional is formed in **u**-dropping (consonant) verbs by adding -**eba** to the basic stem:

| PRESENT | | | BASIC STEM | PRESENT CONDITIONAL | |
|---|---|---|---|---|---|
| **kiku** | 聞く | to hear | **kik-** | **kikeba** | 聞けば |

**ru**-dropping (vowel) verbs add -**reba** to the basic stem:

**taberu** 食べる to eat    **tabe-**    **tabereba**    食べれば

The forms for **kuru** and **suru** are respectively **kureba** and **sureba**. Adjectives form their conditional by adding -**kereba** to the stem:

**takai** 高い high    **taka-**    **takakereba** 高ければ if it is high

A past conditional is formed very simply by adding -**ra** to the past form of a verb or adjective:

| PRESENT | PAST | PAST CONDITIONAL |
|---|---|---|
| **suru** | **shita** | **shitara** |
| する | した | したら |
| to do | | if I did |
| **taberu** | **tabeta** | **tabetara** |
| 食べる | 食べた | 食べたら |
| to eat | | if I ate |
| **iu** | **itta** | **ittara** |
| 言う | 言った | 言ったら |
| to say | | if I said |
| **yasui** | **yasukatta** | **yasukattara** |
| 安い | 安かった | 安かったら |
| cheap | | if it was cheap |

Japanese does not distinguish between ordinary conditions and contrary-to-fact, and does not have special subjunctive forms to conclude a condition. The forms usually follow the natural time sequences, and the conclusion often makes use of the probable mood. This may seem a little difficult at first, but actually it is easier than the Indo-European systems. The following examples will show how conditional sentences are constructed:

**Jisho o tsukaeba wakarimasu.**
辞書を使えばわかります。
[dictionary *obj* if-use understand]
If I use a dictionary, I can understand it.

**Jisho o tsukaeba wakaru deshō.**
辞書を使えばわかるでしょう。
If I used a dictionary, I would probably understand it.

**Jisho o tsukattara wakatta deshō.**
辞書を使かったらわかるでしょう。
If I had used a dictionary, I would have understood it.

**Ame ga fureba ikimasen.**
雨が降れば行きません。
[rain *subj* if-fall not-go]
If it rains, I will not go.

**Ame ga fureba ikanai deshō.**
雨が降れば行かないでしょう。
If it rains, I probably shall not go.

**Shujin ga sore o mireba odoroku deshō.**
主人がそれを見れば驚くでしょう。
[husband *subj* that *obj* if-see surprised probably-is]
If my husband sees it, he will be surprised.

**Shujin ga sore o mitara odoroita deshō.**
主人がそれを見れば驚いたでしょう。
If my husband saw it, he was probably surprised. Or, If my husband
had seen it, he would have been surprised.

**Moshi kare ga itara hanasu deshō.**
もし彼がいたら話すでしょう。
[if he *subj* if-were tell probably-be]
If he were here, I would tell him.

## Liking

The ideas of liking and disliking are expressed in Japanese by shifting
the thought, as in certain European languages, so that the sentence
means, lexically, "such and such is pleasing," "such and such is dis-
pleasing."

 **suki**, a noun, means liking, or an object of liking; **kirai**, also a
noun, means a dislike, or an object of dislike. Both words are used
with **desu** and its tenses, or, more courteous, with (**de**) **gozaimasu**

and its tenses. The subject of the English sentence is set off with **wa**, and the object—the thing liked or disliked—is treated as a grammatical subject with **ga**.

**Ume ga suki desu.**                     **Ume ga suki de gozaimasu.** (polite)
ウメが好きです。                          ウメが好きでございます。
[plums *subj* liking is]
I like plums.

**Kanai wa ringo ga kirai desu.**
家内はリンゴがきらいです。
[my wife as-for apples *subj* disliking is]
My wife does not like apples.

## "Can," "could," "be able"

Japanese has no literal counterpart for such English concepts as "can," "could," "will be able," and so on. There are, instead, several different ways of expressing this idea, the simplest of which is as follows:

(1) Place the basic idea, the process that is to be accomplished, in a normal clause without a polite ending:

**Watashi wa katakana o yomu.**
私はカタカナを読む。
[I as-for katakana *obj* read]
I read katakana.

(2) Place after this the appropriate tense and courtesy form of **koto ga dekiru**:

**Watashi wa katakana o yomu**              **dekimasu** (more polite)
　　**koto ga dekiru.**
私はカタカナを読むことが出来る。できます。
[I as-for katakana *obj* read fact *subj* can-exist]
I am able to read katakana. I can read katakana (one version of the Japanese syllabary).

**Boku wa kanji o yomu koto ga dekimasen.**
僕は漢字を読むことができません。
[I as-for kanji *obj* read fact *subj* cannot-exist]
I am not able to read kanji (Chinese characters).

The grammatical explanation of this idiom is that the word **koto**, meaning thing or situation, becomes the subject of **dekiru**, and the remaining material forms a relative clause modifying **koto**.

A simple idiom indicates ability to speak a language:

**Watashi wa eigo ga dekimasu.**
私は英語ができません。
[I as-for English *subj* am-able]
I can speak English.

**Watashi wa nihongo ga dekimasen.**
私は日本語ができません。
[I as-for Japanese *subj* not-able]
I am not able to speak Japanese.

### "To intend to"
Intention is also expressed in an idiomatic way.

**Boku wa Nihon e iku tsumori desu.**
僕は日本へ行くつもりです。
[I as-for Japan to go intention is]
I intend to go to Japan.

**tsumori** is a noun, and the previous clause, which explains the particular intention, can be understood as a relative clause: the intention that I will go to Japan exists.

### "Ever" and "never"
The idea of "have you ever," "I have never," etc., is expressed in an idiomatic way by the nominalizing expression **koto ga aru**. This is used in a construction parallel to "can" and "could" (see page 95) and intention (see above). You place the main idea in an ordinary sentence without a polite verb ending:

**Murasaki iro no ushi o mita.**
紫色の牛を見た。
[purple color of cow *obj* saw]
I saw a purple cow.

and after this the appropriate forms of **koto ga aru**, according to tense or courtesy.

**Anata wa murasaki iro no ushi o mita koto ga arimasu ka?**
あなたは紫色の牛を見たことがありますか。
[you as-for purple color of cow *obj* saw fact *subj* exists *ques*]
Have you ever seen a purple cow?

**Nihon ryōri o tabeta koto ga arimasen.**
日本料理を食べたことがありません。
[Japanese food *obj* eaten fact *subj* exists-not]
I have never eaten Japanese food.

These expressions can also be understood as relative clauses: the situation in which I have eaten Japanese food does not exist.

**"To have"**
Japanese has two equally common ways of expressing the idea of possession: (1) the verb **motsu**, which by derivation means "to hold," and (2) a paraphrase in which you state that something exists.

**motsu**, "to have" (often with the idea of holding) is normally used in a progressive form:

**Watashi wa okane o motte imasen.**
私はお金を持っていません。
[I as-for *hon*-money *obj* having is-not]
I do not have any money.

Since **motsu** normally means possession in the sense either of holding or actual ownership, it is not used in the many idiomatic ways that the English verb "to have" is. You do not, for example, use **motsu** if you wish to speak of "having time"; instead you use the other construction, as follows.

The second common way of expressing possession is by using the verb meaning "to be"—**aru**—with the postposition **ga** following the object that you have. Thus, the English subject becomes shifted off by itself with **wa**, and the English object becomes the grammatical subject of the clause: as for me, something is.

**Anata ni wa okane ga arimasu ka?**
あなたにはお金がありますか。
[you to as-for *hon*-money *subj* is *ques*]
Do you have any money?

**Sore o suru hima ga arimasen.**
それをするひまがありません。
[that *obj* do time *subj* is-not]
There is no time to do it. I have no time to do it.

## Purpose

Ideas equivalent to "in order to" are expressed by taking the present final form of a verb (see page 42) and placing the words **tame ni** ("for the purpose of") after it.

**Kare wa gakkō ni iku tame ni hatarakimashita.**
彼は学校に行くために働きました。
[he as-for school to go purpose to worked]
He worked in order to go to school.

If the main verb in the sentence has a meaning related to going or coming, this **tame** form is not appropriate. Instead, you take the combining stem of the first verb and place **ni** after it:

**Eiga o mi ni ikimashita.** (from **miru**, "to see")
映画を見に行きました。
[moving-pictures *obj* see to went]
We went to see a movie.

**Kare wa sono koto o hanashi ni kimasu.**
彼はそのことを話に来ます。
he as-for that thing *obj* talk to comes]
He will come to talk about it.

## Quotations, Direct and Indirect Discourse

In English we make a sharp distinction between a direct quotation of what someone has said or thought, and a summarized report of the words. Grammatically, at least, the sentences "John said, 'I will not go'" and "John said that he would not go" are quite different, even though the ultimate meaning may be the same. Japanese does not make this distinction as sharply as English, but in most cases gives the words in the language of the original speaker, without the shifting moods of the English construction.

This construction is used with verbs of saying, asking, thinking, etc., the most common of which are:

| | | | | | | |
|---|---|---|---|---|---|---|
| **iu** | 言う | to say | **omou** | 思う | to think |
| **kangaeru** | 考える | to think | **kiku** | 聞く | to ask |
| **kotaeru** | 答える | to answer | | | |

The original statement is given in the words of the speaker:

**Boku no namae wa Kitagawa desu.**
僕の名前は北川です。
[I of name as-for Kitagawa is]
My name is Kitagawa.

The conjunction **to** (meaning in this case "that" or "thus") is placed at the end of this original statement, and the sentence is finished with the verb of saying or thinking.

**Boku no namae wa Kitagawa desu to kare wa iimashita.**
僕の名前は北川ですと彼は言いました。
[I of name as-for Kitagawa is thus he as-for said]
He said, "My name is Kitagawa." He said that his name was Kitagawa.

Since Japanese has a strong tendency to omit pronouns, you must be careful that you understand the context of the sentence so that its meaning is clear.

An extension of this idiom is very commonly met with in idioms about identity of persons and about hearsay or tradition:

**Yamada-san to iu hito ga kimashita.**
山田さんという人が来ました。
[Yamada-Mr. thus call person *subj* came]
A person named Yamada came. Mr. Yamada came.

**Kore wa Iyeyasu no tsukatta to iu tsukue desu.**
これは家康の作ったという机です。
[this as-for Iyeyasu *subj*\* used thus say desk is]
As for this, it is a desk which Iyeyasu is said to have used. This desk is said to have been used by Iyeyasu.

---

\* **no** indicates the subject of a relative clause.

You should be able to recognize this idiom when you hear it, for it is very common in Japanese, and is used in many places where English usage would find a counterpart unnecessary.

### *shimau*, "to end by"

One of the more common idiomatic Japanese constructions is based upon the verb **shimau**, which means "to finish," "to end," etc. It conveys ideas that we express in English with the words *at last*, *finally* or *to finish doing something*.

When **shimau** is used, the other verb or verbs in the clause are placed in the participle form (see page 45) and **shimau** is used in whatever final form suits tense and courtesy.

> **yomu** 読む to read    **yonde** 読んで participle
>
> **Kono shinbun o yonde shimaimashita ka?**
> この新聞を読んでしまいましたか。
> [this newspaper *obj* reading finished *ques*]
> Have you finished reading this newspaper?

> **neru** 寝る to go to sleep    **nete** 寝て participle
>
> **Akanbō wa nete shimaimashita.**
> 赤ん坊は寝てしまいました。
> [baby as-for sleeping finished]
> The baby finally went to sleep.

> **Gohan\* o tabete shimaimashita.**
> ご飯を食べてしまいました。
> [rice *obj* eating finished]
> He finished the meal.

### "To try"

An easy way of expressing "to try to" or "to try and" involves the verb **miru** (to see). We have a somewhat similar idiom in English: "See if you can . . ." In this construction the main verb or verbs are placed into the participle form (see page 45) and the appropriate final form of **miru** is used.

---

\* **gohan**, literally "rice," is often used to mean a meal, or food, just as in English we use "bread" with the same figurative meaning.

**torikaeru** 取りかえる      **torikaete** 取り替えて   participle
    to exchange, change

**Heya o torikaete mita ga dame deshita.**
部屋を取り替えてみたがだめでした。
[room *obj* changing tried but not-possible was]
We tried to change our room, but it wasn't possible.


**iku** 行く to go    **itte** 行って participle

**Nikkō e itte mimashō.**
日光へ行って見ましょう。
[Nikkō to going let-us-try]
Let us try to reach Nikkō.


**Heya o sagashite mita ga ii no ga nakatta.**
部屋を探してみたが良いのがなかった。
[room *obj* looking-for tried but good one *subj* was-not]
I tried to look for a room, but there were no good ones.

# Clauses and Conjunctions

In Japanese it is not possible to have two equal clauses connected by *and*, as is the case in English. You can not say, for example, "I paid for the hat and left the shop." Japanese would convey such a thought by other possible constructions: "Paying for the hat, I left the shop." "After I paid for the hat, I left the store." These two constructions call for (1) participles, (2) conjunctions.

The use of participles: If you have two clauses (or more) in a sentence, and you do not use conjunctions to join them, the verbs in the earlier clauses are put into the participle form:

**Ginza e itte miyagemono o kaimashō.**
銀座へ行ってみやげ物を買いましょう。
[Ginza to going souvenirs *obj* let-us-buy]
Let's go to the Ginza and buy some souvenirs.

**Annai o yonde setsumei o kikimashita.**
案内を読んで説明を聞きました。
[guide *obj* calling explanation *obj* heard]
We called a guide and heard her explanations. Calling a guide, we heard her explanations.

In such constructions, the relationship between the clauses must be inferred from context. In translation to English, you will sometimes join the two clauses together with *and*; at other times, you will introduce the first clause by *after*, *if*, *when*, or by other such words.

Japanese also has a rich variety of conjunctions for controlling dependent clauses. In all such cases, the conjunction comes at the end of the dependent clause (or clauses), and the dependent material precedes the main clause of the sentence. Most conjunctions are simply particles or postpositions, like those used with nouns and pronouns, but in a few instances they are nouns or frozen verb forms that have lost their verbal meaning. Most conjunctions are used with a final verb form (present, past, probable, present progressive, past progressive, probable progressive—and their negative forms). In such clauses the verb that is governed by the conjunction is often in an abrupt form, rather than in the more courteous locutions with -**masu**. This is not felt to be discourteous, since the main weight of mood and feeling are brought in by the last verb in the sentence—that of the main clause—and this verb may be polite.

The following conjunctions are used with final verb forms:

**to** と usually conveys the ideas of "if," "as," or "when"; it does not convey a strong sense or time or condition, however, but a very slight difference in tone between the two clauses. It can often be translated as "and." It can be used only with a present tense.

**Basu ga tomaru to mina isoide norimashita.**
バスが止まるとみな急いで乗りました。
[bus *subj* stop when all hurrying got-on]
When the bus stopped, we all got on in a hurry.
The bus stopped and we all got on in a hurry.

**Sono michi o iku to kare ni* atta.**
その道を行くと彼に会った。
[the road *obj* go when him to met]
As I went along the road, I met him.

**Nara ni iku to otera o miru koto ga dekimasu.**
奈良に行くとお寺を見ることができました。
[Nara to go if non-temples *obj* see fact *subj* exists]
If you go to Nara, you can see temples.

is also used to "introduce" statements or thoughts, with verbs of saying, thinking, remembering, forgetting, asking, etc. It is placed at the end of the statement, and can be translated as "that." In this case, other tenses than the present can precede **to**.

---

\* **au** normally takes an object with **ni** rather than a direct object with **o**.

**Boku no namae wa Kimura desu to kare wa kotae-mashita.**

僕の名前は木村ですと彼は答えました。

[I of name as-for Kimura is thus he as-for answered]

He answered that his name was Kimura. He answered, "My name is Kimura."

**kara** から means "because." (Do not confuse this with the use described below, with the participle of a verb.)

**Kare wa amerika-jin desu kara nihongo o hanashima-sen.**

彼はアメリカ人ですから日本語を話しません。

[he as-for America-man is because, Japanese *obj* not-speak]

Because he is an American, he does not speak Japanese.

**toki** とき (literally "time"). This means "when" in the sense of "at the time that . . ." or "whenever."

**Kaeru toki kare wa sayōnara to iimashita.**

帰るとき彼はさようならと言いました。

[return time he as-for goodbye thus said]

When he left, he said goodbye.

**Kaeru toki kare wa itsumo sayōnara to iimasu.**

帰るとき彼はいつもさようならといいます。

[return time he as-for always goodbye thus says]

When he leaves, he always says goodbye.

**Sensō ga hajimatta toki boku wa mittsu deshita.**

戦争が始まったよき僕わ三歳でした。

[war *subj* started time I as-for three (years) was]

At the time the war started, I was three years old.

**ga** が may be translated as "but," "although," or as "and." It does not imply a very strong antithesis between the two clauses.

**Kanojo wa utsukushii ga taikutsu desu.**

彼女は美しいが退屈です。

[she as-for beautiful but boring is]

She is good-looking, but boring.

**Nyū Yōku ni ikimashita ga omoshiroi tokoro desu.**
ニューヨークに行きましたが面白い所です。
[New York to went but interesting place is]
I went to New York and it is an interesting place.

**keredomo**
**(or keredo)**
けれども
（けれど）

can be translated as "but." It is stronger than **ga**.

**Kono apāto wa benri da keredo takasugiru.**
このアパートは便利だけれど高すぎる。
[this apartment as-for convenient is but too-expensive]
This apartment is convenient, but too expensive.

**Kimi wa sō iu keredomo boku wa shinjinai.**
君はそう言うけれども僕は信じない。
[you as-for so speak but I as-for do-not-believe]
You say so, but I don't believe it.

**no ni** のに

can usually be translated as "although." It is stronger than **ga**, and usually implies a heavy emotional tone.

**Isshōkenmei benkyō shita no ni kare wa "C" o moraima-**
**shita.**
一生懸命勉強したのに彼は "C" をもらいました。
[diligently study did although — he as-for C *obj* received]
Although he studied hard, he received a "C."

**Matte ita no ni kare wa konakatta.***
待っていたのに彼は来なかった。
[waiting was although — he as-for did-not-come]
Although I had been waiting for him, he did not come.

**no de** ので

means "since" or "because," but is weaker than **kara**.

**Atsui no de oyogi ni ikimashita.**
暑いので泳ぎに行きました。
[hot since — swimming to went]
Since it was hot, I went swimming.

---

* Note that this negative form is built upon the irregular negative stem **ko-** of **kuru**.

**nara** なら

can best be translated as "if." It can be used not only with verbs and adjectives, but also with nouns and pronouns (see page 91).

**Kyōto ni irassharu nara kono densha ni onori nasai.**
京都にいらっしゃるならこの電車にお乗りなさい。
[Kyōto to go if this train (streetcar) on get-on do]
If you go to Kyōto, take this train.

**baai** 場合

is equivalent to *in case* or *when*, in the meaning "if."

**Nihongo o narau baai konki ga hitsuyō desu.**
日本語を習う場合根気が必要です。
[Japanese *obj* learn in-case patience *subj* necessary is]
In case you are studying Japanese, patience is needed. If you are studying Japanese, you have to have patience.

**ato** 後

is equivalent to *after*; it usually takes the past tense.

**Sensō ga owatta ato minna wa shibaraku bonyari shite imashita.**
戦争が終わった後みんなはしばらくぼんやりしていました。
[war *subj* ended after all as-for for-a-long-time dazed doing was]
After the war was over, everyone was dazed for a long time.

When **ato** is used as a postposition with nouns and pronouns, it is used with **no**: **sensō no ato** (after the war).

**mae** 前

is equivalent to *before*; it normally takes the present tense. When used with nouns or pronouns, as a postposition, it also takes **no**.

**Sensō ga hajimaru mae wa subete ga heiwa deshita.**
戦争が始まる前はすべてが平和でした。
[war *subj* begin before as-for everything *subj* peace was]
Before the war began, everything was peaceful.

**Sensō no mae...**
戦争の前…
[war of before . . .]
Before the war . . .

**ue ni** うえに is equivalent to *besides, in addition to.*

**Kare wa osoku kuru ue ni nakanaka kaerimasen.**
彼は遅く来るうえになかなか帰りません。
[he as-for late come besides — readily not return]
Besides coming late, he doesn't return (leave) very readily.

When used as a postposition with a noun or pronoun, and the further postposition **no**, **ue ni** means "on top of," "over," "on":

**Tsukue no ue ni . . .**
机の上に
[desk of surface on . . .]
On top of the desk . . .

**kawari ni**
代わりに
is equivalent to *instead of.*

**Eiga e iku kawari ni uchi de terebi o mimashō.**
映画へ行く代わりにうちでテレビを見ましょう。
[movies to go instead of home at TV *obj* let-us-see]
Instead of going to the movies, let us stay home and watch TV.

When used as a postposition with nouns or pronouns, **no** is added:

**Eiga no kawari ni . . .**
映画の代わりに
[movies of instead of . . .]
Instead of movies . . .

A few conjunctions do not take the final forms of a verb or adjective, but take the participle; these are:

**kara** から meaning "after." Do not confuse this with **kara** meaning "because," which takes a final form.

**Chūshoku o tabete kara dekakemasu.**
昼食を食べてから出かけます。
[lunch *obj* eating after leave]
After eating lunch, I shall leave.

**mo** も          strengthens the opposition inherent within the participle, and can best be translated as "even if," "even though." **tatoe** is sometimes placed at the beginning of the clause:

**(Tatoe) ame ga futte mo asu dekakemasu.**
（たとえ）雨が降ってもあす出かけます。
[even-if rain *subj* falling even-if tomorrow leave]
Even if it is raining tomorrow, I will leave.

Used with two participles, . . . **mo** . . . **mo** means "whether . . . or"; when used with negative verbs, it is often best translated into English as "neither . . . nor."

**Futte mo tette mo dekakemasu.**
降っても照っても出かけます。
[falling whether shining whether leave]
Whether it is raining or shining, I shall leave. I shall leave rain or shine.

**Kare wa naite mo waratte mo imasen.**
彼は泣いても笑ってもいません。
[he as-for crying neither laughing neither is-not]
He is neither crying nor laughing.

The following two conjunctions take the combining stem of a verb:

**nagara**    this is equivalent to English *while*, and like the English
ながら       word can mean either (a) "at the time that," or (b) "even though." It takes a final form when used with an adjective.

**Watashi wa shinbun o yomi\* nagara gohan o tabemasu.**

私は新聞を読みながらご飯を食べます。

[I as-for newspaper *obj* read- while meal *obj* eat]

I eat a meal while reading a newspaper.

**Kare wa wakai nagara shiryobukai.**

彼は若いながら思慮深い。

[he as-for young while prudent]

While he is young, he is prudent. He is prudent even if young. Young as he is, he is prudent.

**ni** に     is equivalent to *in order to*, when used with a verb of going or motion.

**Kare wa shoku o sagashi† ni Tōkyō e kimashita.**

彼は職を探しに東京へ来ました。

[he as-for job *obj* looking-for in-order-to Tōkyō to came]

He came to Tōkyō to look for a job.

These are the most important conjunctions, although there are many other words of various sorts (nouns, particles, verb forms, etc.) that act in the same way as English conjunctions.

We have tabulated these conjunctive words (together with the postpositional particles) on the following pages.

---

\*  From **yomu** (to read).

†  From **sagasu** (to look for).

### Table of Particles

| | With nouns and pronouns | With verbs and adjectives (used as conjunctions) | | |
|---|---|---|---|---|
| | | Final forms | Participles | Combining stem |
| **ga** が | [grammatical subject] *subj* | [Mild antithesis between clauses; sometimes to be translated as "but," sometimes as "and."] | — | — |
| **wa** は | [isolates from remainder of sentence; sometimes to be translated as subject of clauses; sometimes by "as for . . ."] | — | — | — |
| **no** の | of [indicating possession, origin, material of which made, part, apposition, etc.]<br><br>[grammatical subject of dependent clauses] | [Transforms previous material into a noun clause; often ignored in translation] | — | — |
| **o** を | [grammatical object of verb] | | | |
| **kara** から | from; after in certain idioms | because | after | |
| **to** と | with (accompaniment); and (in a limited series) | if, when ("when" in this instance does not indicate time so much as possibility)<br><br>that (used with verbs of thinking, saying, remembering, etc. | | |

| | With nouns and pronouns | With verbs and adjectives (used as conjunctions) | | |
| --- | --- | --- | --- | --- |
| | | Final forms | Participles | Combining stem |
| **ya** や | and (in an un-limited series) | | | |
| **ni** に | to, for (indirect object) | | | in order to |
| | in, on (indicat-ing place) by (with passive or causative verbs, to indi-cate who did the action) | | | |
| | [with verbs meaning to be-come, to meet, to seem, to resemble, etc.] to indicate the direct object | | | |
| **e** へ | to, into (motion towards) | | | |
| **de** で | with, by means of at [equiva-lent logically to the participle "being," often not translated] | | | |
| **ka** か | either . . . or [used in series] | [indicates a ques-tion] | | |
| **mo** も | even, too | | even if | |
| | both . . . and [used in series] | | whether . . . or | |
| | [used with the non-personal pronouns to form the nega-tive range: "no one," "none," etc.] | | neither . . . nor [used in series with a negative verb] | |

| | With nouns and pronouns | With verbs and adjectives (used as conjunctions) | | |
| --- | --- | --- | --- | --- |
| | | Final forms | Participles | Combining stem |
| **de wa** では | [subject of negative verb] | | | |
| **kere-domo** けれども OR **keredo** けれど | | but [stronger antithesis than **ga**] | | |
| **nagara** ながら | | | | while ("during the time that"; "even though") |
| **nara** なら | | if | | |
| **no ni** のに | | although | | |
| **no de** ので | | since, because | | |
| **toki** とき | | when ("at the time that") | | |

# The Language of Courtesy

As we indicated in the first part of these grammatical aids, the degree of politeness or formality that you express in your Japanese is extremely important. We have differentiated four levels of language etiquette: (1) rude, which you should avoid; (2) abrupt-normal, which in some constructions is neutral in tone, and in other grammatical situations is too abrupt to use to a social equal; (3) normal-polite, which you would use on most occasions; (4) very polite, which is somewhat ceremonious, and is best avoided until you are well advanced into Japanese.

The basic ideas behind these levels of language etiquette are these: (1) Vocabulary, grammatical forms, and even constructions that have the same lexical (or observational) meaning can differ quite a bit in their courtesy level. Actually, this concept is present in English, too, where some words are considered all right for colloquial use among friends, but unsuitable for formal writing. (2) When speaking to equals or superiors, you tend to talk-down yourself and your possessions, and to talk-up theirs. For example, when referring to your own wife you use the word **kanai**, which means literally house-person. When speaking of another man's wife, however, you would use the word **oku-san**, which means honorable lady. (3) Directness is to be avoided; everything is to be shaded so that it conveys the connotation "if it please you." For this reason, as we shall see, the direct conjugation forms of the verb and adjective are avoided in some situations, and tempering forms are used (see pages 39, 68); direct tenses are avoided, and probability is invoked; elaborate statements of equivalence (like the French *est-ce que, qu'est-ce que c'est*) are used instead of direct statements; incomplete sentences are commonly used. Women, generally speaking, are required to use politer levels of language etiquette than are men.

### Honorific Verbs and Adjectives

We have already covered the conjugational forms of verbs and adjectives, as well as the polite verb forms in -**masu** (and other forms) that can be substituted for them. We shall simply list these forms in the tables on this page and on page 116.

### Table of Abrupt and Polite Verb Forms in Common Use

**aruku** (to walk)   **aruki-**(combining stem)   **aruka-** (negative stem)

|  | ABRUPT | POLITE |
|---|---|---|
| Present | **aruku**<br>歩く<br>I walk | **arukimasu**<br>歩きます<br>I walk |
| Negative | **arukanai**<br>歩かない<br>I do not walk | **arukimasen**<br>歩きません<br>I do not walk |
| Present progressive | **aruite iru**<br>歩いている<br>I am walking | **aruite imasu**<br>歩いています<br>I am walking |
| Negative | **aruite inai**<br>歩いていない<br>I am not walking | **aruite imasen**<br>歩いていません<br>I am not walking |
| Past | **aruita**<br>歩いた<br>I walked | **arukimashita**<br>歩きました<br>I walked |
| Negative | **arukanakatta**<br>歩かなかった<br>I did not walk | **arukimasen deshita**<br>歩きませんでした<br>I did not walk |
| Past progressive | **aruite ita**<br>歩いていた<br>I was walking | **aruite imashita**<br>歩いていました<br>I was walking |
| Negative | **aruite inakatta**<br>歩いていなかった<br>I was not walking | **aruite imasen deshita**<br>歩いていませんでした<br>I was not walking |

|  | ABRUPT | POLITE |
|---|---|---|
| Probable | **arukō** OR **aruku darō**<br>歩こう、歩くだろう<br>let us walk | **arukimashō** OR **aruku deshō**<br>歩きましょう、歩くでしょう<br>let us walk |
| Negative | **arukanai darō**<br>歩かないだろう<br>let us not walk | **arukanai deshō**<br>歩かないでしょう<br>let us not walk |
| Probable progressive | **aruite iru darō**<br>歩いているだろう<br>is probably walking | **aruite iru deshō**<br>歩いているでしょう<br>is probably walking |
| Negative | **aruite inai darō**<br>歩いていないだろう<br>is probably not walking | **aruite inai deshō**<br>歩いていないでしょう<br>is probably not walking |
| Participle | **aruite**<br>歩いて<br>walking | |
| Negative | **arukanakute** OR **arukanaide**<br>歩かなくて、歩かないで<br>not walking | |
| Imperative (commands) | [omitted] | **aruite kudasai; aruki nasai**<br>歩いてください；歩きなさい<br>please walk |
| Negative | | **arukanaide kudasai**<br>歩かないでください<br>please do not walk |

The abrupt verb forms are used in the following situations, each of which is discussed in detail elsewhere:

(1) At the end of sentences. This form is somewhat abrupt, and you would be best advised to avoid it.
(2) In clauses, with certain conjunctions. This is normal use.
(3) In relative clauses. This is normal use.

(4) As modifying adjectives. This is really a form of relative clause, and is normal use.

The polite verb forms are used in the following situations:

(1) At the end of sentences. This is normal use, and is the practice you should follow.
(2) In clauses, with certain conjunctions. This, too, is normal use, although the abrupt forms may be used here, too.

Observe that the polite forms are not normally used in relative clauses or as adjectives.

**Table of Abrupt and Polite Adjective Forms in Common Use**

| | ABRUPT | NORM. POLITE | VERY POLITE |
|---|---|---|---|
| Present | shiroi<br>白い<br>is white | shiroi no desu<br>白いのです<br>is white | shirō gozaimasu<br>白うございます<br>is white |
| Negative | shiroku nai<br>白くない<br>is not white | shiroku arimasen<br>白くありません<br>is not white | shirō gozaimasen<br>白うございません<br>is not white |
| Past | Shirokatta<br>白かった<br>was white | shiroi no deshita<br>白いのでした<br>was white | shirō gozaima-<br>shita<br>白うございました<br>was white |
| Negative | shiroku nakatta<br>白くなかった<br>was not white | shiroku arimasen<br>deshita<br>白くありませんで<br>した<br>was not white | shirō gozaimasen<br>deshita<br>白うございません<br>でした<br>was not white |
| Probable | shiroi darō<br>白いだろう<br>is probably white | shiroi deshō<br>白いでしょう<br>is probably white | shirō gozaimashō<br>白うございまし<br>ょう<br>is probably white |
| Negative | shiroku nai darō<br>白くないだろう | shiroku nai deshō<br>白くないでしょう | shirō gozaimasen<br>deshō<br>白うございません<br>でしょう |

| | ABRUPT | NORM. POLITE | VERY POLITE |
|---|---|---|---|
| Adverb | **shiroku**<br>白く<br>whitely | | |
| Continuative | **shirokute** or **shiroku**<br>白くて、白く<br>being white | | |
| Negative | **shiroku nakute**<br>白くなくて<br>not being white | | |

With adjectives, the abrupt forms are used as follows:

(1) At the end of sentences. As with verbs, this is abrupt, and is best avoided.
(2) To modify nouns. This is normal usage.
(3) Used predicatively, as final words before conjunctions, or in relative clauses. This, too, is normal use. The probables are not used in relative clauses.

The polite adjectival forms are used:

(1) At the end of sentences, predicatively. They are not used within clauses or sentences.

The notions of giving and receiving are particularly associated with etiquette and respect: you give something down to an inferior, and something up to a superior. Hence, a superior or equal gives something down to you, while you give things up to him. This results in the somewhat peculiar situation that the choice of verb of giving tells you who the speaker is. **sashiageru** is used to indicate services that the first person renders to another; it literally means "to lift up." **kudasaru** (literal meaning "to hand down") or **itadaku** (literal meaning "to place upon one's head") indicate services that someone else (second or third person) renders to the first person.

**Kono hon o yonde sashiagemashō ka?**
この本を読んで差し上げましょうか。
[this book *obj* reading probably-giving *ques*]
Shall I read this book to you?

**Tanabe-san ni hon o kashite itadakimashita.**
田辺さんに本を貸していただきました。
[Tanabe-Mr. by book *obj* lending I-received]
I received a book from Mr. Tanabe as a loan. Mr. Tanabe lent me a book.

**Enpitsu o kudasai.**
鉛筆をください。
[pencil *obj* please-give]
Please give me the pencil.

The following list includes a few of the more common verbs that are used with honorific intent for most situations; you should recognize them when you hear them.

| PLAIN VERB | SPEAKING OF YOURSELF | SPEAKING OF SOMEONE ELSE |
|---|---|---|
| **iku** OR **yuku**<br>行く<br>to go | **mairu**<br>参る | **irassharu**<br>いらっしゃる |
| **iu**<br>言う<br>to say | **mōshiageru**<br>(LIT. to raise speech)<br>申し上げる | **ossharu**<br>おっしゃる |
| **miru**<br>見る<br>to see | **haiken suru**<br>拝見する | **goran nasaru**<br>ご覧なさる |
| **taberu**<br>食べる<br>to eat | **itadaku**<br>(LIT. to receive)<br>いただく | **meshiagaru**<br>(LIT. food rising)<br>召し上がる |
| **yaru**<br>やる<br>to give | **sashiageru**<br>(LIT. lift up)<br>差し上げる | **kudasaru**<br>(LIT. to hand down)<br>くださる |
| **iru**<br>いる<br>to be | **iru**<br>いる | **irassharu**<br>いらっしゃる |

Another way of expressing a sense of respect or formality is by using the true passive (see page 63) form of the verb, instead of the active form that the sense would seem to demand:*

| Taberaremashita ka? | Ikaremasu† ka? |
|---|---|
| 食べられましたか。 | 行かれますか。 |
| [been-eaten *ques*] | [be-gone *ques*] |
| Have you eaten? | Are you going? |

Incomplete sentences are sometimes used to convey a sense of respect for the person spoken to:

**Ii otenki de gozaimasu ga.**
いいお天気でございますが。
[good *hon*-weather *subj* is but]
It is fine weather [if it please you].

## Honorific Nouns and Pronouns

Nouns, too, can be used in an honorific sense. The prefixes **o** (usually with words of Japanese origin) or **go** (usually with words of Chinese origin) are attached to a noun when you are talking about someone else's possessions, activities, or situations, or wish to preserve a respectful tone.

| ii otenki | oyu |
|---|---|
| いいお天気 | お湯 |
| [good *hon*-weather] | [*hon*-warm-water] |
| good weather | warm water |

**Otegami o mimasen deshita.**
お手紙を見ませんでした。
[non-letter *obj* not-see was]
I did not see your letter.

You would not speak of your own letter as **otegami**, since the **o** is honorific, but simply as **tegami**.

In some words these honorific prefixes are so standardized that they have lost any honorific meaning, and are best simply thought of as part of the word:

---

\* For recognition only.

† In Japanese, intransitive verbs like *die*, *go*, etc., can be passive in form.

**ocha** お茶 tea　　　　**gohan** ご飯 rice, food

Honorifics are quite idiomatic in Japanese, for there are some nouns which do not take honorific prefixes. As a result, you had better not make your own honorifics, but be content to use forms that you have learned or heard in conversation.

If you are referring to someone else's relations, you use a different vocabulary than if you are speaking about your own:

| Your Own | | | Someone Else's | | | |
|---|---|---|---|---|---|---|
| | | | POLITE | | VERY POLITE | |
| wife | **kanai** | 家内 | **oku-san** | 奥さん | **oku-sama** | 奥様 |
| father | **chichi** | 父 | **otō-san** | お父さん | **otō-sama** | お父様 |
| mother | **haha** | 母 | **okā-san** | お母さん | **okā-sama** | お母様 |
| son | **musuko** | 息子 | **musuko-san** | 息子さん | **go shisoku** | ご子息 |
| daughter | **musume** | 娘 | **musume-san** | 娘さん | **ojō-sama** | お嬢様 |

We have covered pronouns in some detail in the earlier part of the book. Let us recapitulate by saying that

**watashi**　　　**watashitachi** or **watashidomo**
私　　　　　　私たち、私ども
I　　　　　　　we

**anata**　　　　**anatatachi** or **anatagata**
あなた　　　　あなたたち、あなた方
you　　　　　you

**kare**　　　　　**karera** or **anokata**
彼　　　　　　彼ら、あの方
he　　　　　　(they, MASC.)

**kanojo**　　　　**kanojotachi**
彼女　　　　　彼女たち
she　　　　　　(they, FEM.)

**anokata**　　　　**anokatatachi**
あの方　　　　あの方たち
he or she　　　(they, FEM., MASC.)

are the polite forms that you would normally use, while **boku** (I), **kimi** (you, SING.), **bokutachi** (we), **kimitachi** (you, PL.) are less formal words that you would use to intimates or members of your family.

# Word Order

Word order in Japanese is very important and is relatively rigid, especially when particles are sometimes omitted in rapid colloquial speech and word order is the criterion for determining the meaning of a sentence.

If all the elements of a clause are present, the following is the basic pattern of word order:

dissociated material (if any)—subject—indirect object— direct object—verb form

If particles are properly given, this word order need not be rigidly observed, except that the verb always comes at the end of the clause or sentence.

Expressions of time usually precede expressions of place. They may both precede the subject, whether they are isolated by the dissociating particle **wa**, or whether they have other particles, or none at all. They may also be placed immediately before the verb. Adverbs of manner or degree normally immediately precede the verb.

Adjectives precede the noun they modify.

Particles and conjunctions always follow the material they control.

Relative clauses always precede the word they modify. Within themselves relative clauses follow the same rules of word order as sentences.

Dependent clauses always come first in a sentence.

The following sentences will show how words and elements are placed in ordinary sentences:

| **Kesa** | **boku** | **wa** | **kare** | **ni** | **omiyage** | **o** | **ageta.** |
|---|---|---|---|---|---|---|---|
| けさ | 僕 | は | 彼 | に | おみや | げ をあげた。 | |
| adv. | subject | part. | indir.-obj. | part. | dir.-obj. | part. | verb |

[this-morning I as-for him to souvenir *obj* gave]
I gave him a souvenir this morning.

**Kino boku ga atarashii uchi ni hikkoshita no de,**
きのう 僕 が 新しい うち に 引っ越した の で、

adv. subject part. adjective noun part. verb conj.

[yesterday I *subj* new { Place where } moved since,
{ house to }

**kare wa kyō isoide yatte kite,**
彼 は 今日 急いで やって 来て、

subject part. adv. verb verb verb
                        participle participle participle

he as-for today hurrying bringing-coming

**boku ni kare no kaita e o kuremashita.**
僕 に 彼 の 描いた 絵 を くれました。

indir. part, subject part. verb noun dir.- verb
obj.                                  obj.

relative clause

[I to he *subj* painted picture *obj* gave]

Because I moved into a new home yesterday, he came in a hurry today, and gave me a picture that he had painted.

The first material within large brackets is a dependent clause, ending in **no de**; the phrase **kare no kaita** is a relative clause.

# Forming Questions

Most Japanese complete sentences can be turned into questions by adding at their very end the particle **ka**, which is the equivalent of a question mark.

POSITIVE
**Kore wa anata no desu.**
これはあなたのです。
[this as-for you of is]
This is yours.

INTERROGATIVE
**Kore wa anata no desu ka?**
これはあなたのですか。
[this as-for you of is *ques*]
Is this yours?

The particle **ne**, which is also placed at the end of a sentence, is the equivalent of *n'est-ce pas* or *nicht wahr*, and can be translated as "isn't it," or "don't you think," or something similar.

**Ii tenki desu ne.**
いい天気ですね。
[good weather is not-so]
It's fine weather, isn't it?

Questions that occur in the probable mood (see page 48) often do not require the particle **ka** in order to be questions, although in this situation an affirmative answer is usually anticipated. Rising tone at the end of the sentence indicates a question.

**Ashita iku deshō?**
あした行くでしょう？
[tomorrow go probably]
We shall probably go tomorrow?

Questions are also made with interrogative pronouns and certain adverbs or conjunctions:

| | | |
|---|---|---|
| **itsu desu ka?** | いつですか。 | when is it? |
| **doko desu ka?** | どこですか。 | where is it? |

| | | |
|---|---|---|
| **nan desu ka?** | 何ですか。 | what is it? |
| { **dochira\* desu ka?** | どちらですか。 | } which one is it? |
| { **dore† desu ka?** | どれですか。 | |
| **dare desu ka?** | 誰ですか。 | who is it? |
| **nanji desu ka?** | 何時ですか。 | what time is it? |

In most cases, such questions use the particle **ka** at their end.

---

\* Which of two.
† Which of more than two.

# Numbers and Counting Objects

The Japanese numerical system is extremely complex, and it cannot be encompassed within this brief introduction to Japanese grammar. The most that this manual can do is survey briefly a few of the more important features in the use of numbers, so that you will understand the principles behind such numbers as you are likely to hear. In all probability you will not be able to use the numerical system correctly without further study in a more advanced grammar, but if you follow the hints given in this book you will at least be understood.

Japanese has two systems of numbers, one of which is native, and the other of which is Chinese in origin:

| Japanese | | | | | Chinese | |
|---|---|---|---|---|---|---|
| INDEPENDENT FORM | | | JOINING FORM | | | |
| 1 | hitotsu | 一つ | hito- | ひと | ichi | 一 |
| 2 | futatsu | 二つ | futa- | ふた | ni | 二 |
| 3 | mittsu | 三つ | mi- | み | san | 三 |
| 4 | yottsu | 四つ | yo- | よ | shi (or yon) | 四 |
| 5 | itsutsu | 五つ | itsu- | いつ | go | 五 |
| 6 | muttsu | 六つ | mu- | む | roku | 六 |
| 7 | nanatsu | 七つ | nana- | なな | shichi | 七 |
| 8 | yattsu | 八つ | ya- | や | hachi | 八 |
| 9 | kokonotsu | 九つ | kokono- | ここの | ku (or kyū) | 九 |
| 10 | tō | 十 | tō- | とお | jū | 十 |

After 10, only Chinese numerals are used. Their forms are regular, except for occasional phonetic changes that are optional.

| | | |
|---|---|---|
| 11 | jū-ichi | 十一 |
| 12 | jū-ni | 十二 |
| 13 | jū-san | 十三 |
| 14 | jū-shi | 十四 |
| 15 | jū-go | 十五 |

| 16 | **jū-roku** | 十六 |
|---|---|---|
| 17 | **jū-shichi** | 十七 |
| 18 | **jū-hachi** | 十八 |
| 19 | **jū-ku** | 十九 |
| 20 | **ni-jū** | 二十 |
| 21 | **nijū-ichi** | 二十一 |
| 30 | **san-jū** | 三十 |
| 40 | **shijū** or **yon-jū** | 四十 |
| 100 | **hyaku** | 百 |
| 108 | **hyaku-hachi** | 百八 |
| 200 | **ni-hyaku** | 二百 |
| 1000 | **is-sen** or **sen** | 一千、千 |
| 10,000 | **ichi-man** | 一万 |

Although the true Chinese number for four is **shi**, the Japanese number, **yon**, is often substituted for **shi** (in some combinations) since **shi** is also the Japanese root meaning death, and its use was considered inauspicious.

Use of these two sets of numbers is complex and highly idiomatic, as you will see in later sections of this chapter. At this point we shall indicate only a few of the situations in which each type of numeral is used.

The Japanese forms are used:

(a) In statements of age:

**Hanako no toshi wa ikutsu desu ka? Muttsu desu.**
花子のとしはいくつですか。六つです。
[Hanako of years as-for how-many is *ques*. Six is.]
How old is Hanako? She is six. (She is six years old.)

(b) When mentioning quantities of objects (not persons):

**Mittsu kudasai. Futatsu shika arimasen.**
三つください。二つしかありません。
[Three please-give. Two only are-not]
Please give me three. There are only two.

We shall describe this use of Japanese numerals in more detail in the section describing classifiers, at which point it will be seen that the situation on this usage is very complex.

The Chinese forms are used when talking about measures of time, distance, and money, with the following words:

| | | | | | | |
|---|---|---|---|---|---|---|
| **ji** | 時 | o'clock | **nen** | 年 | year |
| **en** | 円 | yen | **shaku** | 尺 | foot |
| **fun** | 分 | minute | **kai** | 階 | story of a building |

**Kakitomeryō o awasete go hyaku nana jū en desu.**
書留料を合わせて五百七十円です。
[Registration-fee *obj* including five hundred and seventy yen is]
Including the registration fee, it is five hundred and seventy yen.

**fun** undergoes phonetic changes when it is combined with numerals. These changes are indicated in the table of classifiers and numerals on page 129.

## Classifiers

One of the most difficult features of the numerical system is the concept of classifiers, or special words that are used with numbers to show the categories of different things. In English we speak of three head of cattle, two hands of cards, two sheets of paper, five pieces of cake, and so on. Japanese has carried this idea much farther, so that most articles must be described in terms of words like head, hand, sheet, and so on. Thus, one speaks of five persons of carpenters, two cylinders of pencils, two surfaces of paper, coins, or coats, and so on.

There are many of these classifiers in use in Japanese, but we shall list only the most common:

| | | |
|---|---|---|
| **nin** | 人 | used with human beings |
| **hiki** | 匹 | used with animals |
| **hon** | 本 | with long, slender objects like sticks, pencils, arms, etc. |
| **satsu** | 冊 | with books or magazines |
| **mai** | 枚 | with flat things like paper, coins, clothing |
| **hai** | 杯 | cups full, pots full, etc. |
| **chaku** | 着 | suits of clothing |
| **soku** | 足 | pairs of shoes and stockings |
| **kire** | 切れ | slice of meat, fish, cake, etc. |
| **ko** | 個 | item, used generally |

Some of these classifiers are used with the Chinese numbers, while others are used with the Japanese combining forms. Phonetic

| | 1 | 2 | 3 | 4 | 5 | 6 | 7 | 8 | 9 | 10 | how many |
|---|---|---|---|---|---|---|---|---|---|---|---|
| **nin** 人, used with humans | hitori ひとり | futari ふたり | san-nin 三人 | yo-nin 四人 | go-nin 五人 | roku-nin 六人 | shichi-nin or nana-nin 七人 | hachi-nin 八人 | ku-nin or kyū-nin 九人 | jū-nin 十人 | nan-nin 何人 |
| **hiki** 匹, used with animals | ip-piki 一匹 | ni-hiki 二匹 | san-biki 三匹 | yon-hiki 四匹 | go-hiki 五匹 | rop-piki 六匹 | shichi-hiki or nana-hiki 七匹 | hachi-hiki 八匹 | kyū-hiki 九匹 | jip-piki 十匹 | nan-biki 何匹 |
| **hon** 本, used with long slender objects | ip-pon 一本 | ni-hon 二本 | san-bon 三本 | yon-hon 四本 | go-hon 五本 | rop-pon 六本 | shichi-hon or nana-hon 七本 | hachi-hon or ha-ppon 八本 | kyū-hon 九本 | jip-pon 十本 | nan-bon 何本 |
| **satsu** 冊, used with books, magazines, etc. | is-satsu 一冊 | ni-satsu 二冊 | san-satsu 三冊 | yon-satsu 四冊 | go-satsu 五冊 | roku-satsu 六冊 | shichi-satsu or nana-satsu 七冊 | has-satsu 八冊 | kyū-satsu 九冊 | jis-satsu 十冊 | nan-satsu 何冊 |
| **mai** 枚, with flat sheetlike objects | ichi-mai 一枚 | ni-mai 二枚 | san-mai 三枚 | yo-mai or yon-mai 四枚 | go-mai 五枚 | roku-mai 六枚 | nana-mai 七枚 | hachi-mai 八枚 | kyū-mai 九枚 | jū-mai 十枚 | nan-mai 何枚 |

| | 1 | 2 | 3 | 4 | 5 | 6 | 7 | 8 | 9 | 10 | how many |
|---|---|---|---|---|---|---|---|---|---|---|---|
| **hai** 杯, cups full etc. | **ip-pai** 一杯 | **ni-hai** 二杯 | **san-bai** 三杯 | **yon-hai** 四杯 | **go-hai** 五杯 | **roku-hai** or **rop-pai** 六杯 | **nana-hai** 七杯 | **hachi-hai** or **hap-pai** 八杯 | **kyū-hai** 九杯 | **jip-pai** 十杯 | **nan-bai** 何杯 |
| **chaku** 着, suits of clothing | **it-chaku** 一着 | **ni-chaku** 二着 | **san-chaku** 三着 | **yon-chaku** 四着 | **go-chaku** 五着 | **roku-chaku** 六着 | **nana-chaku** 七着 | **hat-chaku** 八着 | **kyū-chaku** 九着 | **jit-chaku** 十着 | **nan-chaku** 何着 |
| **soku** 足, pairs of shoes, etc | **is-soku** 一足 | **ni-soku** 二足 | **san-zoku** 三足 | **yon-soku** 四足 | **go-soku** 五足 | **roku-soku** 六足 | **nana-soku** 七足 | **has-soku** 八足 | **kyū-soku** 九足 | **jis-soku** 十足 | **nan-zoku** 何足 |
| **kire** 切れ, slice of | **hito-kire** 一切れ | **futa-kire** 二切れ | **mi-kire** 三切れ | **yon-kire** 四切れ | **go-kire** 五切れ | **rok-kire** 六切れ | **nana-kire** 七切れ | **hak-kire** 八切れ | **kyū-kire** 九切れ | **jik-kire** 十切れ | **nan-kire** 何切れ |
| **ko** 個, table, used with almost anything | **ik-ko** 一個 | **ni-ko** 二個 | **san-ko** 三個 | **yon-ko** 四個 | **go-ko** 五個 | **rok-ko** 六個 | **nana-ko** 七個 | **hak-ko** 八個 | **kyū-ko** 九個 | **jik-ko** 十個 | **nan-ko** 何個 |
| **fun** 分, minute | **ip-pun** 一分 | **ni-fun** 二分 | **san-pun** 三分 | **yon-pun** 四分 | **go-fun** 五分 | **rop-pun** 六分 | **shichi-fun** or **nana-fun** 七分 | **hachi-fun** 八分 | **kyū-fun** 九分 | **jip-pun** 十分 | **nan-pun** 何分 |

changes are frequent with these forms, as you can see from the tables on pages 128 and 129

Where a definite classifier is not called for, Japanese usually applies the independent forms of the Japanese range of numbers: **hitotsu, futatsu, mittsu**, etc. If you wish, you can use this group as numbers whenever you talk about things or objects (though not about human beings). This may not always be correct, but it will always be intelligible.

Numbers are used grammatically in three ways: (1) alone, (2) after the noun, or (3) with **no** before the noun.

(1) **san-bon**
三本
three

(2) **enpitsu san-bon**
鉛筆三本
[pencils three-cylinders]
three pencils

(3) **san-bon no enpitsu**
三本の鉛筆
[3-cylinders of pencils]
three pencils

**Ringo ga mittsu aru.**
リンゴが三つある。
[apples *subj* three are]
There are three apples.

**Mittsu no ringo ga aru.**
三つのリンゴがある。
[three of apples *subj* are]
There are three apples.

**Ringo o mittsu kudasai.**
リンゴを三つください。
[apples *obj* three give]
Please give me three apples.

**Kōhii ip-pai ikaga desu ka?**
コーヒー一杯いかがです。
[coffee one-cup how is *ques*]
How about a cup of coffee?

**Ip-pai kudasai.**
一杯ください。
[one-cup give]
Please give me a cup (of coffee).

## Dates and Telling Time

Two systems of giving the year are used in Japan. The Japanese way is to speak of the –th year of whatever emperor is reigning. Thus, 2010 would be Heisei (the era of the Emperor Akihito) twenty-two:

**Heisei nijū-nin nen**
平成二十二年
[Heisei two ten two year]
the 22nd year of Heisei

One can also use the Christian system:

**ni-sen jū nen**
二千十年
[two thousand ten year]
2010

The months are formed by the Chinese numerals and the word **gatsu**, meaning "month," in combinations:

**ichigatsu** 一月 January
**nigatsu** 二月 February
**sangatsu** 三月 March
**shigatsu** 四月 April

etc. The days of the month are slightly irregular in formation:

| | | |
|---|---|---|
| 1st | **tsuitachi** | 一日 |
| 2nd | **futsu-ka** | 二日 |
| 3rd | **mik-ka** | 三日 |
| 4th | **yok-ka** | 四日 |
| 5th | **itsu-ka** | 五日 |
| 6th | **mui-ka** | 六日 |
| 7th | **nano-ka** | 七日 |
| 8th | **yō-ka** | 八日 |
| 9th | **kokono-ka** | 九日 |
| 10th | **tō-ka** | 十日 |
| 11th | **jū-ichi-nichi** | 十一日 |
| 12th | **jū-ni-nichi** | 十二日 |
| 13th | **jū-san-nichi** | 十三日 |
| 14th | **jū-yok-ka** | 十四日 |
| 15th | **jū-go-nichi** | 十五日 |
| 16th | **jū-roku-nichi** | 十六日 |

| 17th | jū-shichi-nichi | 十七日 |
|------|------|------|
| 18th | jū-hachi-nichi | 十八日 |
| 19th | jū-ku-nichi | 十九日 |
| 20th | hatsu-ka | 二十日 |
| 21st | nijū-ichi-nichi | 二十一日 |
| 22nd | nijū-ni-nichi | 二十二日 |
| 23rd | nijū-san-nichi | 二十三日 |
| 24th | nijū-yok-ka | 二十四日 |
| 25th | nijū-go-nichi | 二十五日 |
| 26th | nijū-roku-nichi | 二十六日 |
| 27th | nijū-shichi-nichi | 二十七日 |
| 28th | nijū-hachi-nichi | 二十八日 |
| 29th | nijū-ku-nichi | 二十九日 |
| 30th | sanjū-nichi | 三十日 |
| 31st | sanjū-ichi-nichi | 三十一日 |

**Kyō wa nan-nichi desu ka?**
今日は何日ですか。
[today as-for what-day is *ques*]
What day is today?

**Kyō wa ni-sen jū nen rokugatsu tō-ka desu.**
今日は2010年6月10日です。
[today as-for 2000 10 year June 10th is]
Today is June 10, 2010.

The hours are formed by using the Chinese numerals and the word **ji**:

| | | | | | | |
|------|------|------|------|------|------|------|
| **ichi-ji** | 1時 | one o'clock | **shichi-ji** | 7時 | seven o'clock |
| **ni-ji** | 2時 | two o'clock | **hachi-ji** | 8時 | eight o'clock |
| **san-ji** | 3時 | three o'clock | **ku-ji** | 9時 | nine o'clock |
| **yo-ji** | 4時 | four o'clock | **jū-ji** | 10時 | ten o'clock |
| **go-ji** | 5時 | five o'clock | **jū-ichi-ji** | 11時 | eleven o'clock |
| **roku-ji** | 6時 | six o'clock | **jū-ni-ji** | 12時 | twelve o'clock |

A.M. is expressed by placing **gozen** before the number of the hour; P.M., by placing **gogo** before the hour. Noon is **hiru**. Midnight is **mayonaka**.

The minutes are expressed by a combination of the Chinese numerals and the word **fun**; phonetic combinations occur in several numbers.

| | | | | | | |
|---|---|---|---|---|---|---|
| 1 minute | **ip-pun** | 1分 | 13 minutes | **jū-san-pun** | 13分 |
| 2 minutes | **ni-fun** | 2分 | 14 minutes | **jū-yon-pun** | 14分 |
| 3 minutes | **san-pun** | 3分 | 15 minutes | **jū-go-fun** | 15分 |
| 4 minutes | **yon-pun** | 4分 | 16 minutes | **jū-rop-pun** | 16分 |
| 5 minutes | **go-fun** | 5分 | 17 minutes | **jū-shichi-fun** | 17分 |
| 6 minutes | **rop-pun** | 6分 | 18 minutes | **jū-hachi-fun** | 18分 |
| 7 minutes | **shichi-fun** | 7分 | | (or **jū-hap-pun**) | |
| | (or **nana-fun**) | | 19 minutes | **jū-kyū-fun** | 19分 |
| 8 minutes | **hachi-fun** | 8分 | 20 minutes | **nijip-pun** | 10分 |
| | (or **hap-pun**) | | 21 minutes | **nijū-ip-pun** | 21分 |
| 9 minutes | **kyū-fun** | 9分 | 30 minutes | **sanjip-pun** | 30分 |
| 10 minutes | **jip-pun** | 10分 | | (or **han**) | |
| 11 minutes | **jū-ichi-fun** | 11分 | | (meaning "half") | |
| | (or **jū-ip-pun**) | | 31 minutes | **sanjū-ip-pun** | 31分 |
| 12 minutes | **jū-ni-fun** | 12分 | 40 minutes | **yonjip-pun** | 40分 |
| | | | 50 minutes | **gojip-pun** | 50分 |

The intermediate numbers are formed regularly in the same manner as the 20 minute series.

To express minutes after, you use the word **sugi** after the number of minutes; to express minutes before, you use the word **mae** after the number of minutes.

**Nanji desuka?**
何時ですか。
[what time is *ques*]
What time is it ?

**Shichi-ji desu.**
7時です。
[seven-o'clock is]
It is seven.

**Gogo shichi-ji go-fun mae (sugi) desu.**
午後7時5分前(すぎ)です。
[P.M. seven-o'clock five-minutes before (after) is]
It is five minutes before (after) seven P.M. It is 6:55 (7:05) P.M.

**Gozen shichi-ji han desu.**
午前7時半です。
[A.M. seven-o'clock half is]
It is half past seven A.M.

# Idiomatic Expressions

Japanese is rich in idiomatic expressions of courtesy, most of which do not lend themselves easily to grammatical analysis. It would be impossible to list more than a few of them. Others can be found in a good phrase book or a more extensive grammar.

**okinodoku desu**
お気の毒です
I am very sorry [to hear it].

**goran nasai**
ごらんなさい
Look!

**arigatō [gozaimashita]**
ありがとう（ございました）
Thank you.

**omachidō sama**
ごちそう様
I'm sorry to have kept you waiting.

**okagesama de**
おかげ様で
Thanks to you. (usually untranslated)

**ojama itashimashita**
おじゃましました
Sorry to have bothered you.
   (when leaving someone's house)

**ohayō gozaimasu**
おはようございます
Good morning.

**oyasumi nasai**
おやすみなさい
Good night.

**konban wa**
こんばんは
Good evening.

**konnichi wa**
こんにちは
Good day. Good morning. Hello.

**sayōnara**
さようなら
Au revoir. Goodbye.

**gomen nasai**
ごめんなさい
Excuse me. I am sorry. Pardon me.

**sumimasen**
すみません
Excuse me. I am sorry. Pardon me.

**shitsurei itashimasu**
失礼いたしました
Excuse me—I must leave. May I
   come in?

**chotto haiken**
ちょっと拝見
May I look at it?

**dō itashimashite**
どういたしまして
You're welcome. Not at all.

**hajimemashite**
初めまして
Pleased to meet you.

**dōzo yoroshiku**
どうぞよろしく
Pleased to meet you.

**shikata ga nai**
しかたがない
I'm sorry, but there's nothing one can do about it. What can you do about it?

**omedetō gozaimasu**
おめでとうございます
Congratulations.

**dōmo**
どうも
[usually understood from context as part of a sentence: Thank you, not at all, I'm sorry, I'm embarrassed, etc.].

# Appendix 1: Japanese Pronunciation

Japanese is relatively easy for an English speaker to pronounce, since there are very few sounds that do not appear in English, and Japanese sound combinations are simple. The following table will summarize the most important features:

**a**   as in f*a*ther

**ā**   as in f*a*ther, but held longer

**b**   as in *b*at

**ch** as in *ch*at

**d**   as in *d*ental

**e**   as in m*e*n

**ē**   as in m*e*n, but held longer

**f**   unlike English *f*. Formed by bringing the lower lip up so that it almost touches the upper lip, then holding the position and trying to say an *f*. (English *f*, on the other hand, is formed by bringing the lower lip up to touch the teeth.) If you cannot manage the Japanese *f*, the English *f* will always be intelligible.

**g**   as in *g*o. In the middle of words and in the particle **ga** in standard Japanese, *g* is often pronounced like *ng* in so*ng*. But an English *g* is always intelligible and correct.

**h**   as in *h*ome. In the syllable *hi*, however, *h* is pronounced like a harsh *sh* or *ch* in German *ich*.

**i**   as in benz*i*ne.

**ii**   as in benz*i*ne, but held longer

**j**   as in *j*et

**k**   as in *c*at

**m**   as in *m*at

**n**   as in *n*et. At the end of words *n* is often pronounced by Tōkyō speakers as if it were halfway between *n* and *ng* (in si<u>ng</u>). An ordinary *n* is always intelligible, and is not incorrect.

**o**   as in n*o*tify. Pronounce this as a single pure sound, not as a diphthong; English *o* is a diphthong of *o-u*.

**ō**   as in n*o*tify, but held longer

**p**   as in s*p*ry. Do not make an *h* sound after the sound *p*, as we do in English in words like <u>p</u>in or <u>p</u>et.

**r**   unlike English *r*. Made with a single flip of the tip of the tongue against the ridge behind your upper front teeth. It often sounds like a *d* to an English ear.

**s**   as in *s*ay

**sh** as in *she*

**t** as in *stop*. Do not make an *h* sound after the sound *t*, as we do in English in words like tin or ten.

**u** as in *food*. Do not round the corners of your mouth when you make this sound; draw them back.

**ū** as in *food*, but held longer

**w** as in *wash*

**y** as in *yard*. *y* is a consonant, not a vowel.

**z** as in *zone*. The combination *zu* is pronounced *dzu*.

There are certain special situations and general points that deserve special mention. (1) The long vowels **ā, ē, ii, ō, ū** are considered different letters from the short vowels, and must be given their full value. An incorrect long or short vowel will change the meaning of a word: **toru** means "to take"; **tōru**, "to pass."

(2) In some situations the letters **i** and **u** are not fully sounded. This usually occurs between voiceless consonants (**p, ch, ts, s, k, sh**) or after a voiceless consonant at the end of a phrase. In such instances they are whispered, or not pronounced at all. To give a few common examples: -**masu** is pronounced **mas**; -**mashita** is pronounced **mashta**; **desu** is pronounced **des**; **deshita** is pronounced **deshta**. Imitate your CD or software on individual words and situations here, since this is subject to many variations and exceptions.

(3) Observe double consonants very closely in Japanese; they are not simply curiosities of spelling, as they often are in English, but are meaningful. You will change the meaning of a word by making an error in this respect: **kite**, for example, means "coming"; **kitte** means "postage stamp."

(4) Do not stress certain syllables and swallow others; Japanese does not have a strong stress system like English. Instead, pronounce each sound clearly and distinctly, with a moderate, even stress. Pitch of the voice, though it does enter into Japanese, is best ignored by a beginner, since it is difficult to master, and is probably not clearly indicated in the dictionaries available to you. In most situations it is not important.

### Possible Combinations and Sound Shifts

The table on page 139 indicates the range of permitted primary vowel and consonant combinations. As you will note there are five basic vowels—**a, i, u, e, o**—and fourteen consonants—**k, s, t, n, h, m, y, r, w, g, z, d, b, p.** The following combinations are not permitted in Japanese: **si** (instead, use **shi**); **ti** (instead, use **chi**); **tu** (instead, use **tsu**); **hu** (instead, use **fu**) ; **yi, ye, wi, wu, we** (for which the ordinary vowels are used); **wo** (which has a special symbol but is pronounced **o**); **zi** (instead, use **ji**); **di** (instead, use **ji**); **du** (instead, use **zu**).

This table is not as difficult as it may seem at first glance, since it is nothing but the Japanese syllabary in transcription. You will find it useful in two areas. (1) Japanese, like English, borrows words from foreign languages very easily. Therefore, if you are at a loss for the name of a Western article in Japanese, there is a good chance that you will be understood if you simply say the the English word slowly, ending each syllable with a vowel, making the foreign word fit the phonetic pattern of Japanese. Examples: lemonade, **remonēdo**; cheese, **chiizu**; vanilla, **banira**; coffee, **kōhii**; fuse, **hyūzu**; valve, **barubu**; etc. As you will observe, Japanese has no l-sound, and uses **r** in its place; consonant clusters are avoided by inserting neutral vowels; all syllables end with a vowel or **-n**. (2) In verb or adjective conjugation, the stem of the word may end in a consonant in which there is a phonetic change. For example, in the verb **matsu**, "to wait," the stem is **mat-**. The present form ends in **-u**, producing **matsu**, since *matu is impossible. The joining stem ends in **-i**, producing **machi**, since *mati is impossible. The negative stem ends in **-a**, producing **mata**, which is possible. Similarly, for **dasu**, to take, the joining stem would end in **-i**, and would become **dashi-**.* The past of **-masu** becomes **-mashita**, since the past is formed by adding **-ita** to the stem **-mas-**.

---

* An earlier form of Romanization, which you may meet occasionally, did not follow the phonetic pronunciation but adhered to the phonemic structure of the language; from this point of view the **ts** of **tsu** and the **ch** of **chi** are simply positional variants of **t**. This system would write **matu-**, **mati-**, and **dasi-**. Thus, the name of the famous Japanese vessel was spelled as Titibu Maru, even though it was pronounced as Chichibu Maru.

|  | -a | -i | -u | -e | -o |
|---|---|---|---|---|---|
| [no consonant] | a あ | i い | u う | e え | o お |
| **k-** | ka か | ki き | ku く | ke け | ko こ |
| **s-** | sa さ | shi し | su す | se せ | so そ |
| **t-** | ta た | chi ち | tsu つ | te て | to と |
| **n-** | na な | ni に | nu ぬ | ne ね | no の |
| **h-** | ha は | hi ひ | fu ふ | he へ | ho ほ |
| **m-** | ma ま | mi み | mu む | me め | mo も |
| **y-** | ya や |  | yu ゆ |  | yo よ |
| **r-** | ra ら | ri り | ru る | re れ | ro ろ |
| **w-** | wa わ | (i) い | (u) う | (e) え | o を |
| **g-** | ga が | gi ぎ | gu ぐ | ge げ | go ご |
| **z-** | za ざ | ji じ | zu ず | ze ぜ | zo ぞ |
| **d-** | da だ | ji じ | zu ず | de で | do ど |
| **b-** | ba ば | bi び | bu ぶ | be べ | bo ぼ |
| **p-** | pa ぱ | pi ぴ | pu ぷ | pe ぺ | po ぽ |
| **n** ん |  |  |  |  |  |

# Appendix 2: Conjugation Tables for Japanese Verbs

## Consonant or *U*-dropping Verbs

| | | kaku 書く to write | |
|---|---|---|---|
| Basic Stem | | **kaki-** 書き | |
| Negative Stem | | **kaka-** 書か | |
| Participle | | **kaite*** 書いて | |
| Neg. Participle | | **kakanakute, kakanaide** 書かなくて、書かないで | |

| | | POSITIVE | NEGATIVE |
|---|---|---|---|
| **A** | Present | **kaku** 書く | **kakanai** 書かない |
| | Past | **kaita** 書いた | **kakanakatta** 書かなかった |
| **B** | Probable | **kakō** 書こう | **kakanai darō** 書かないだろう |
| **R** | Progressive | **kaite iru** 書いている | **kaite inai** 書いていない |
| **U** | Command | **kake!** 書け書くな | **kaku na!** 書くな |
| **P** | Conditional -eba | **kakeba** 書けば | **kakanakereba** 書かなければ |
| **T** | Conditional -tara | **kaitara** 書いたら | **kakanakattara** 書かなかったら |
| | Passive | **kakareru** 書かれる | **kakarenai** 書かれない |
| | Causative | **kakaseru** 書かせる | **kakasenai** 書かせない |
| **P** | Present | **kakimasu** 書きます | **kakimasen** 書きません |
| | Past | **kakimashita** 書きました | **kakimasen deshita** 書きませんでした |
| **O** | Probable | **kakimashō** 書きましょう | **kakanai deshō** 書かないでしょう |
| **L** | Progressive | **kaite imasu** 書いています | **kaite imasen** 書いていません |
| **I** | Command | **kaite kudasai!** 書いて下さい | **kakanaide kudasai!** 書かないで下さい |
| **T** | Passive | **kakaremasu** 書かれます | **kakaremasen** 書かれません |
| **E** | Causative | **kakasemasu** 書かせます | **kakasemasen** 書かせません |

---

\* While all **ru**-dropping verbs form the participle by dropping -**ru** and adding -**te**, the consonant or **u**-dropping verbs vary slightly depending on the final consonant of the word. As with **kaku** above, all **u**-dropping verbs whose final consonant is -**k** drop -**ku** and add -**ite**. **Kiku** (listen), for example, becomes **kiite**, and **maku** (roll) becomes **maite**. For the rules for these changes, see p 138.

## *Ru*-dropping Verbs

| taberu 食べる to eat | | |
|---|---|---|
| Basic Stem | **tabe-** 食べ | |
| Negative Stem | **tabe-** 食べ | |
| Participle | **tabete** 食べて | |
| Neg. Participle | **tabenakute, tabenaide** 食べなくて、食べないで | |

| | | POSITIVE | NEGATIVE |
|---|---|---|---|
| | Present | **taberu** 食べる | **tabenai** 食べない |
| | Past | **tabeta**<br>食べた | **tabenakatta**<br>食べなかった |
| A | Probable | **tabeyō**<br>食べよう | **tabenai darō**<br>食べないだろう |
| B | Progressive | **tabete iru**<br>食べている | **tabete inai**<br>食べていない |
| R | Command | **tabero!** 食べろ | **taberu na!** 食べるな |
| U | Conditional -**eba** | **tabereba**<br>食べれば | **tabenakereba**<br>食べなければ |
| P | Conditional -**tara** | **tabetara**<br>食べたら | **tabenakattara**<br>食べなかったら |
| T | Passive | **taberareru**<br>食べられる | **taberarenai**<br>食べられない |
| | Causative | **tabesaseru**<br>食べさせる | **tabesasenai**<br>食べさせない |
| | Present | **tabemasu**<br>食べます | **tabemasen**<br>食べません |
| P | Past | **tabemashita**<br>食べました | **tabemasen deshita**<br>食べませんでした |
| O | Probable | **tabemashō**<br>食べましょう | **tabemasen deshō**<br>食べませんでしょう |
| L | Progressive | **tabete imasu**<br>食べています | **tabete imasen**<br>食べていません |
| I | Command | **tabete kudasai!**<br>食べて下さい | **tabenaide kudasai!**<br>食べないで下さい |
| T | Passive | **taberaremasu**<br>食べられます | **taberaremasen**<br>食べられません |
| E | Causative | **tabesasemasu**<br>食べさせます | **tabesasemasen**<br>食べさせません |

## Irregular Verb

| suru する to do | | |
|---|---|---|
| Basic Stem | **shi-** し | |
| Negative Stem | **shi-** し | |
| Participle | **shite** して | |
| Neg. Participle | **shinakute, shinaide** しなくて、しないで | |

| | | POSITIVE | NEGATIVE |
|---|---|---|---|
| **A** | Present | **suru** する | **shinai** しない |
| | Past | **shita** した | **shinakatta** しなかった |
| **B** | Probable | **shiyō** しよう | **shinai darō** しないだろう |
| **R** | Progressive | **shite iru** している | **shite inai** していない |
| | Command | **shiro!** しろ | **suru na!** するな |
| **U** | Conditional -**eba** | **sureba** すれば | **shinakereba** しなければ |
| **P** | Conditional -**tara** | **shitara** したら | **shinakattara** しなかったら |
| **T** | Passive | **sareru** される | **sarenai** されない |
| | Causative | **saseru** させる | **sasenai** させない |
| **P** | Present | **shimasu** します | **shimasen** しません |
| | Past | **shimashita** しました | **shimasen deshita** しませんでした |
| **O** | Probable | **shimashō** しましょう | **shimasen deshō** しませんでしょう |
| **L** | Progressive | **shite imasu** しています | **shite imasen** していません |
| **I** | Command | **shite kudasai!** して下さい | **shinaide kudasai!** しないで下さい |
| **T** | Passive | **saremasu** されます | **saremasen** されません |
| **E** | Causative | **sasemasu** させます | **sasemasen** させません |

## Irregular Verb

### kuru 来る to come

| | |
|---|---|
| Basic Stem | **ki-** 来 |
| Negative Stem | **ko-** 来 |
| Participle | **kite** 来て |
| Neg. Participle | **konakute, konaide** 来なくて、来ないで |

| | | POSITIVE | NEGATIVE |
|---|---|---|---|
| A | Present | **kuru** 来る | **konai** 来ない |
| | Past | **kita** 来た | **konakatta** 来なかった |
| B | Probable | **kiyō**<br>来よう | **konai darō**<br>来ないだろう |
| R | Progressive | **kite iru** 来ている | **kite inai** 来ていない |
| | Command | **koi!** 来い | **kuru na!** 来るな |
| U | Conditional -**eba** | **kureba**<br>来れば | **konakereba**<br>来なければ |
| P | Conditional -**tara** | **kitara**<br>来たら | **konakattara**<br>来なかったら |
| T | Passive | **korareru** 来られる | **korarenai** 来られない |
| | Causative | **kosaseru** 来させる | **kosasenai** 来させない |
| P | Present | **kimasu** 来ます | **kimasen** 来ません |
| | Past | **kimashita**<br>来ました | **kimasen deshita**<br>来ませんでした |
| O | Probable | **kimashō**<br>来ましょう | **kimasen deshō**<br>来ないでしょう |
| L | Progressive | **kite imasu**<br>来ています | **kite imasen**<br>来ていません |
| I | Command | **kite kudasai!**<br>来て下さい | **konaide kudasai!**<br>来ないで下さい |
| T | Passive | **koraremasu**<br>来られます | **koraremasen**<br>来られません |
| E | Causative | **kosasemasu**<br>来させます | **kosasemasen**<br>来させません |

# A Glossary of Grammatical Terms

This section is intended to refresh your memory of English grammatical terms or to clear up difficulties you may have had in understanding them. Before you work through the Japanese grammar, you should have a reasonably clear idea what the parts of speech and parts of a sentence are. This is not for reasons of pedantry, but simply because it is easier to talk about grammar if we agree upon terms. Grammatical terminology is as necessary to the study of grammar as the names of car parts are to mechanics.

## The Parts of Speech

English words can be divided into eight important groups: nouns, adjectives, articles, verbs, adverbs, pronouns, prepositions, and conjunctions. The boundaries between one group and another are sometimes vague and ill-felt in English, but a good dictionary can help you make decisions in questionable cases. Always bear in mind that the way a word is used in a sentence may be just as important as the nature of the word itself in deciding what part of speech the word is.

**Nouns.** Nouns are the words for things of all sorts, whether these things are real objects that you can see, or ideas, or places, or qualities, or groups, or more abstract things. Examples of words that are nouns are *cat, vase, door, shrub, wheat, university, mercy, intelligence, ocean, plumber, pleasure, society, army.* If you are in doubt whether a given word is a noun, try putting the word *my*, or *this*, or *large* (or some other adjective) in front of it. If it makes sense in the sentence, the chances are that the word in question is a noun.

**Adjectives.** Adjectives are the words that delimit or give you specific information about the various nouns in a sentence. They tell you size, color, weight, pleasantness, and many other qualities. Such words as *big, expensive, terrible, insipid, hot, delightful, ruddy, informative* are all clear adjectives. If you are in any doubt whether a certain word is an adjective, add -er to it, or put the word *more* or *too* in front of it. If it makes good sense in the sentence, and does not end in -ly, the chances are that it is an adjective. (Pronoun-adjectives will be described under pronouns.)

**ARTICLES**. There are only two kinds of articles in English, and they are easy to remember. The definite article is *the* and the indefinite article is *a* or *an*.

**VERBS**. Verbs are the words that tell what action, or condition, or relationship is going on. Such words as *was, is, jumps, achieved, keeps, buys, sells, has finished, run, will have, may, should pay*, and *indicates* are all verb forms. Observe that a verb can be composed of more than one word, as *will have* and *should pay*, above; these are called compound verbs. As a rough guide for verbs, try adding -ed to the word you are wondering about, or taking off an -ed that is already there. If it makes sense, the chances are that it is a verb. (This does not always work, since the so-called strong or irregular verbs make forms by changing their middle vowels, like *spring, sprang, sprung*.)

**ADVERBS**. An adverb is a word that supplies additional information about a verb, an adjective, or another adverb. It usually indicates time, manner, place, or degree. It tells you who, or when, or where, or to what degree things are happening. Such words as *now, then, there, not, anywhere, never, somehow, always, very*, and most words ending in -ly are ordinarily adverbs.

**PRONOUNS**. Pronouns are related to nouns, and take their place. (Some grammars and dictionaries group pronouns and nouns together as substantives.) They mention persons, or objects of any sort without actually giving their names.

There are several different kinds of pronouns, (1) Personal pronouns: by a grammatical convention *I, we, me, mine, us, ours* are called first-person pronouns, since they refer to the speaker; *you* and *yours* are called second-person pronouns, since they refer to the person addressed; and *he, him, his, she, hers, they, them, theirs* are called third-person pronouns since they refer to the things or persons discussed. (2) Demonstrative pronouns: *this, that, these, those*. (3) Interrogative, or question, pronouns: *who, whom, what, whose, which*. (4) Relative pronouns, or pronouns that refer back or relate to something already mentioned: *who, whom, that, which*. (5) Others: *some, any, anyone, no one, other, whichever, none*, etc.

Pronouns are difficult for us, since our categories are not as clear as in some other languages, and we often use the same words for what foreign-language speakers see as different situations. First, our interrogative and relative pronouns overlap, and must be separated in translation. The easiest way is to observe whether a question is involved in the sentence. Examples: "Which [int.] do you like?" "The inn, which [rel.] was not far from Tōkyō, had a restaurant." "Who [int.] is there?" "I don't know who [int.] was there." "The porter who [rel.] took our bags was Number 2132." This may seem to be a trivial difference to an English speaker, but in some languages, like Japanese, it is very important.

Secondly, there is an overlap between pronouns and adjectives. In some cases the word *this*, for example, is a pronoun; in other cases it is an adjective. This also holds true for *his, its, her, any, none, other, some, that, these, those*, and many other words. Note whether the word in question stands alone or is associated with another word. Examples: "This [pronoun] is mine." "This [adj.] taxi has no springs." Watch out for the word *that*, which can be a pronoun, adjective, or conjunction. And remember that *my, your, our*, and *their* are always adjectives.

**PREPOSITIONS.** Prepositions are the little words that introduce phrases that tell about condition, time, place, manner, association, degree, and similar topics. Such words as *with, in, beside, under, of, to, about, for*, and *upon* are prepositions. In English, prepositions and adverbs overlap, but, as you will see by checking in your dictionary, there are usually differences of meaning between the two uses.

**CONJUNCTIONS.** Conjunctions are joining-words. They enable you to link words or groups of words into larger units, and to build compound or complex sentences out of simple sentence units. Such words as *and, but, although*, or, *unless* are typical conjunctions. Although most conjunctions are easy enough to identify, the word *that* should be watched closely to see that it is not a pronoun or an adjective.

### Words about Verbs
Verbs are responsible for most of the terminology in this short grammar. The basic terms are:

**CONJUGATION.** In many languages verbs fall into natural groups, according to the way they make their forms. These groupings are called conjugations, and are an aid to learning grammatical structure.

**INFINITIVE.** This is the basic form that most dictionaries give for verbs in most languages, and in most languages it serves as the basis for classifying verbs. In English (with a very few exceptions) it has no special form. To find the infinitive for any English verb, just fill in this sentence: "I like to ...... (walk, run, jump, swim, carry, disappear, etc.)." The infinitive in English is usually preceded by the word *to*.

**TENSE.** This is simply a formal way of saying "time." In English we think of time as being broken into three great segments: past, present, and future. Our verbs are assigned forms to indicate this division, and are further subdivided for shades of meaning. We subdivide the present time into the present (I walk) and present progressive (I am walking); the past into the simple past (I walked), progressive past (I was walking), perfect or present perfect (I have walked), past perfect or pluperfect (I had walked); and future into simple future (I shall walk) and future progressive (I shall be walking). These are the most common English tenses. Other languages, like Japanese, may not have exact counterparts.

**PRESENT PARTICIPLES, PROGRESSIVE TENSES.** In English the present participle always ends in -ing. It can be used as a noun or an adjective in some situations, but its chief use is in forming the so-called progressive tenses. These are made by putting appropriate forms of the verb "to be" before a present participle: For "to walk" [an infinitive], for example, the present progressive would be: I am walking, you are walking, he is walking, etc.; past progressive, I was walking, you were walking, and so on.

**PAST PARTICIPLES, PERFECT TENSES.** The past participle in English is not formed as regularly as is the present participle. Sometimes it is constructed by adding -ed or -d to the present tense, as *walked, jumped, looked, received*; but there are many verbs where it is formed less regularly: *seen, been, swum, chosen, brought*. To find it, simply fill out the sentence "I have ......." putting in the verb form that your ear tells you is right for the particular verb. If you speak grammatically, you will have the past participle.

Past participles are sometimes used as adjectives: "Don't cry over spilt milk." Their most important use, however, is to form the system of verb tenses that are called the perfect tenses: present perfect (or perfect), past perfect (or pluperfect), etc. In English the present perfect tense is formed with the present tense of "to have" and the past participle of a verb: I have walked, you have run, he has begun, etc. The past perfect is formed, similarly, with the past tense of "to have" and the past participle: I had walked, you had run, he had begun. Most of the languages you are likely to study have similar systems of perfect tenses, though they may not be formed in exactly the same way as in English.

**PRETERIT, IMPERFECT.** Many languages have more than one verb tense for expressing an action that took place in the past. They may use a perfect tense (which we have just covered), or a preterit, or an imperfect. English, although you may never have thought about it, is one of these languages, for we can say "I have spoken to him" [present perfect], or "I spoke to him" [simple past], or "I was speaking to him" [past progressive]. These sentences do not mean exactly the same thing, although the differences are subtle and are difficult to put into other words.

While usage differs a little from language to language, if a language has both a preterit and an imperfect, in general the preterit corresponds to the English simple past (I ran, I swam, I spoke), and the imperfect corresponds to the English past progressive (I was running, I was swimming, I was speaking). If you are curious to discover the mode of thought behind these different tenses, try looking at the situation in terms of background action and point action. One of the most important uses of the imperfect is to provide a background against which a single point action can take place. For example, "When I was walking down the street [background, continued over a period of time, hence past progressive or imperfect], I stubbed my toe [an instant or point of time, hence a simple past or preterit]."

**AUXILIARY VERBS.** Auxiliary verbs are special words that are used to help other verbs make their forms. In English, for example, we use forms of the verb "to have" to make our perfect tenses: I have seen, you had come, he has been, etc. We also use "shall" or "will" to make our future tenses: I shall pay, you will see, etc. French, German, Spanish, and Italian also make use of auxiliary verbs, but although the same general concept is present, the use of auxiliaries differs very much from one language to another, and you must learn the practice for each language.

**PASSIVE.** In some languages, like Latin, there is a strong feeling that an action or thing that is taking place can be expressed in two different ways. One can say, A does-something-to B, which is "active"; or B is-having-something-done-to-him by A, which is "passive." We do not have a strong feeling for this classification of experience in English, but the following examples should indicate the difference between an active and a passive verb: Active: "John is building a house." Passive: "A house is being built by John." Active: "The steamer carried the cotton to England." Passive: "The cotton was carried by the steamer to England." Bear in mind that the formation of passive verbs and the situations where they can be used vary enormously from language to language. This is one situation where you usually cannot translate English word for word into another language and make sense.

## Miscellaneous Terms

**COMPARATIVE, SUPERLATIVE.** These two terms are used with adjectives and adverbs. They indicate the degree of strength within the meaning of the word. *Faster, better, earlier, newer, more rapid, more detailed, more suitable* are examples of the comparative in adjectives, while *more rapidly, more recently, more suitably* are comparatives for adverbs. In most cases, as you have seen, the comparative uses -er or *more* for an adjective, and *more* for an adverb. Superlatives are those forms which end in -est or have "most" placed before them for adjectives, and *most* prefixed for adverbs: *most intelligent, earliest, most rapidly, most suitably.*

**IDIOM.** An idiom is an expression that is peculiar to a language, the meaning of which is not the same as the literal meaning of the individual words composing it. Idioms, as a rule, cannot be translated word by word into another language. Examples of English idioms: "Take it easy." "Don't beat around the bush." "It turned out to be a Dutch treat." "Can you tell time in Italian?"

### The Parts of the Sentence

SUBJECT, PREDICATE. In grammar every complete sentence contains two basic parts, the subject and the predicate. The subject, if we state the terms most simply, is the thing, person, or activity talked about. It can be a noun, a pronoun, or something that serves as a noun. A subject would include, in a typical case, a noun, the articles or adjectives which are associated with it, and perhaps phrases. Note that in complex sentences, each part may have its own subject.

The predicate talks about the subject. In a formal sentence the predicate includes a verb, its adverbs, predicate adjectives, phrases, and objects—whatever happens to be present. A predicate adjective is an adjective that happens to be in the predicate after a form of the verb to be. Example: "Apples are red."

In the following simple sentences subjects are in italics, predicates in italics and underlined. "*Green apples are bad for your digestion.*" "When *I go to Japan*, I *always stop in Tōkyō*." "*The man with the handbag is traveling to Kōbe*."

DIRECT AND INDIRECT OBJECTS. Some verbs (called transitive verbs) take direct and/or indirect objects in their predicates; other verbs (called intransitive verbs) do not take objects of any sort. In English, except for pronouns, objects do not have any special forms, but in languages that have case forms or more pronoun forms than English, objects can be troublesome.

The direct object is the person, thing, quality, or matter that the verb directs its action upon. It can be a pronoun, or a noun, perhaps accompanied by an article and/or adjectives. The direct object always directly follows its verb, except when there is also an indirect object present, which comes between the verb and the object. Prepositions do not go before direct objects. Examples: "The cook threw green onions into the stew." "The border guards will want to see your passport tomorrow." "Give it to me." "Please give me a glass of red wine."

The indirect object, as grammars will tell you, is the person or thing for or to whom the action is taking place. It can be a pronoun or a noun with or without article and adjectives. In most cases the words "to" or "for" can be inserted before it, if they are not already there. Examples: "Please tell me the time." "I wrote her a letter from Ōsaka." "We sent Mr. Tanizaki fifty yen." "We gave the most energetic guide a large tip."

**CLAUSES : INDEPENDENT, DEPENDENT, RELATIVE.** Clauses are the largest components/that go to make up sentences./ Each clause, in classical grammar, is a combination of subject and predicate./ If a sentence has one subject and one predicate,/ it is a one-clause sentence. If it has two or more subjects and predicates,/ it is a sentence of two or more clauses./

There are two kinds of clauses: independent (principal) and dependent (subordinate) clauses./ An independent clause can stand alone ;/ it can form a logical, complete sentence./ A dependent clause is a clause/that cannot stand alone;/it must have another clause with it to complete it./

A sentence containing a single clause is called a simple sentence./ A sentence with two or more clauses may be either a complex or a compound sentence./ A compound sentence contains two or more independent clauses,/and/these independent clauses are joined together with *and* or *but*./ A complex sentence is a sentence/that contains both independent and dependent clauses./

A relative clause is a clause/that begins with a relative pronoun: *who, whom, that, which*./ It is by definition a dependent clause,/ since it cannot stand by itself.

In English these terms are not very important except for rhetorical analysis,/since all clauses are treated very much the same in grammar and syntax. In some foreign languages, like Japanese, however, these concepts are important,/and they must be understood,/since all clauses are not treated alike. [Each clause in this section has been isolated by slashes.]

## Special Terms Describing Japanese Grammar

In our description of Japanese grammar, we have used a few special terms that may not be familiar to the reader. These terms have been explained within the text as they arose, but we shall repeat brief definitions here. For more detail consult the pages indicated.

**STEMS**. In some languages, like Japanese, Latin, or classical Greek, where endings or prefixes are used to make new forms, there is often a basic element (which cannot normally be used by itself) to which the endings or prefixes are added. This basic element is called a stem. The concept of the stem is not too significant in the Germanic portion of English, but traces of it can be found in many of the words and concepts borrowed from Latin and Greek. In the words *lexicon*, *lexical*, *lexically*, *lexicographer* the form *lexic-* is a stem; it cannot be used by itself, but it can be used to form a range of words (or ideas) by adding new material.

In Japanese, verbs and adjectives are best analyzed in terms of stems. The ultimate form to which you can go in a verb is the so-called basic stem (see page 37), which is used as a substructure for all other stems and forms. We describe three other stems in this brief survey: the combining stem, which is used when you join one verb to another or make ordinary tenses (see page 39); the negative stem, which is used to make negative forms (see page 53); and the conditional stem, which we have mentioned only for recognition (see page 92).

Adjectives, for the purpose of this brief survey, have only one stem, a basic stem, from which all other forms are made (see page 65).

**PROBABLE FORMS**. Verbs and adjectives have sets of forms that are used to indicate probability, doubt, and similar areas of meaning which we express by more complex constructions in English. "We shall probably come," "I think we shall come," and similar ideas are expressed by special forms which are made as regularly as other verb forms (see page 48).

**FINAL AND MEDIAL FORMS**. Certain verb and adjective forms can be used without other forms to complete them; they are thereby independent verbs upon which complete sentences are founded. According to the genius of Japanese, these forms are placed in final position: at the end of a sentence, at the end of a clause, or at the end of modifying material. These forms include present, present progressive, past,

past progressive, probable, and probable progressive. Certain other forms, however, do not have sufficient strength to be used without other verbs to complete their sense. These forms are placed within the sentence, and cannot appear as a final element. Such forms include the true verb or adjective conditional, the participle if used without a completing form, the various stems, and for the adjective the continuative or suspending form (see page 70). (This, of course, refers to exact speech; colloquially, exceptions may be made.)

This may seem like an alien concept, but actually we have the same practice, though to a somewhat lesser extent, in English. A sentence that contains only a present participle or an infinitive or a past participle is not considered a complete sentence. Example: "Walking down the street . . .," "To be or not to be . . .," "Gone out of my life. . . ."

**POSTPOSITIONS AND PARTICLES.** Particles are small units of speech (found in certain languages like Japanese, and to a lesser extent, classical Greek) that indicate relationships within a sentence, but do not coincide with the basic English parts of speech. In Japanese they perform the offices of prepositions and conjunctions, and also serve as pointers to show material that has been set off from the rest of the sentence and to indicate subjects and direct objects. Since they are always placed after the material they govern, they are also called postpositions.

**CLASSIFIER.** In Japanese and Chinese, objects that are counted are normally listed according to certain units, which vary according to the object itself. This is best understood by our comparable (though much less important) English practice: two sheets of paper, five head of cattle, three sticks of wood, etc. These terms *sheets, head, sticks* have nothing to do with quantity or with special type of material; they are simply a convention in counting. But while classifiers are exceptional in English, they are extremely important in Japanese.

# Index

The following abbreviations have been used in this index: *conj*, for conjunction and *def.* for definition. Japanese words appear in boldface and their English equivalents in parentheses. Where no true equivalent is possible, as in the case of some particles, the material in parentheses is not a translation but an identification, such as "particle" or "nominalizer."